Horace Bushnell

The vicarious Sacrifice

Vol. II

Horace Bushnell

The vicarious Sacrifice
Vol. II

ISBN/EAN: 9783337192983

Printed in Europe, USA, Canada, Australia, Japan

Cover: Foto ©ninafisch / pixelio.de

More available books at **www.hansebooks.com**

UNIFORM EDITION

OF THE SELECT WORKS OF

HORACE BUSHNELL, D.D.

Each 1 vol. 12mo, per vol. $1.50.

AND TO INCLUDE

CHRISTIAN NURTURE.
SERMONS FOR THE NEW LIFE.
CHRIST AND HIS SALVATION.
SERMONS ON LIVING SUBJECTS.
VICARIOUS SACRIFICE. Vol. I.
VICARIOUS SACRIFICE. Vol. II.
NATURE AND THE SUPERNATURAL.

SCRIBNER, ARMSTRONG & CO.,

PUBLISHERS,

743 and 745 Broadway, New York.

THE VICARIOUS SACRIFICE,

GROUNDED IN PRINCIPLES

INTERPRETED

BY HUMAN ANALOGIES.

BY
HORACE BUSHNELL.

IN TWO VOLUMES.

VOL. II.

NEW YORK:
SCRIBNER, ARMSTRONG & CO.
1877.

COPYRIGHT BY
MARY A. BUSHNELL,
1877.

JOHN F. TROW & SON,
PRINTERS AND BOOKBINDERS,
205-213 *East 12th St.*,
NEW YORK.

ADVERTISEMENT.

At the time the present volume was published, the author announced his intention that it should eventually take the place of Parts III. and IV. of his treatise, published eight years before, and entitled, "The Vicarious Sacrifice,"—the whole, so recomposed, to bear that title. This purpose was somewhat shaken by the urgency of some of his friends, who were unwilling to lose any part of that earlier book. Since his death, this feeling has been expressed anew and very generally; indeed, among the many men of learning and judgment, and yet of varying shades of opinion, who have been consulted on this point, there has been but one voice as to the loss it would be, intellectually and historically, were the proposed omissions to be made. It seems, therefore, to those in whose hands the decision was left, a duty to retain both volumes intact, approaching, however, their author's original design as closely as possible, by publishing them as the first and second volumes of one work, and under one title—the first treating of the sacrifice of Christ especially in its relations to the character of man, and so to his redemption; the second regarding it rather as related to the mind and purposes of God.

Such an arrangement is, on the whole, more nearly in accord with the author's mind than that which he first proposed; for he, in no sense, regarded the later work as contradictory to, or inconsistent with, the former, as he distinctly states in the Introduction. The new view was not, to his eyes, one side of the old, but beyond and above it. It was as if another lens had been added to the telescope, or a new height reached. Looking down and back then, as it were, upon those earlier steps by which his mind had climbed, it was not unnatural that he should somewhat underrate their importance, as related to the history of his own mind and to the thinking of others.

The chief objection to retaining both volumes without change, is the occasional recurrence, in the second, of matter contained in the latter half of the first. It is hoped the reader will bear in mind the original plan, as accounting for this repetition, which no revision but that of the constructing hand could now remedy.

In an appendix will be found notes left by the author, containing new matter, whereby he hoped to throw light upon certain difficult points of his subject. The whole work, as it now stands in these two volumes, represents his progressive and completed view, so far as he was able to express it, of what was, during the greater part of his life, the absorbing theme of his study and thought.—Ed.

CONTENTS.

INTRODUCTION.

IN WHAT way led to this revision, *Page* 12. The moral view of atonement asserted even more completely, 14. Novelty excused, 16. How all doctrines have to pass a change of form when they come into the human molds of thought, 18. Reasons why this doctrine of Christ requires revision, 23.

Page.

CHAPTER I.—FORGIVENESS AND PROPITIATION, WITHOUT EXPIATION . 33
The one principle that underlies the subject, 34.

I.

Forgiveness by God and by men coincide in the New Testament, one set forth by the other, 35. Negative forgivenesses, 36. Difficulties that are real, 37. How forgivenesses fail, 39. Two things necessary, sympathy with and cost made for the subject, 40–41. Examples for illustration, 42, 45, 46. We require in forgiveness to be ourselves propitiated, 48. In this we have the tragic element of our virtue, 49.

II.

The analogy of our own propitiations, 50. Applied to God, 52. Not that Christ dies for the reaction of it, 53. God loves his adversary already, 54. God's holiness not too inflexible, 55. God's office in government no objection, 56. Our analogies only show that we propitiate ourselves, 57. No implication dishonorable to God, 59. God's propitiation above time, 60.

III.

Scripture statement of propitiation, 63. *Usus loquendi* of the altar word, 64. Old Testament sacrifices, 66. Statute concerning blood, 68. How these old forms are related to Christ's sacrifice, 71. The Propitiation thus set forth, 72.

IV.

Objection to all propitiations however conceived, 73. Propitiations from eternity, 74. Another solution, 76. Not supposed that God has reluctances here to overcome, 77. An ideal of God that must have great value, 78.

V.—(WITHOUT EXPIATION.)

What now to be thought of expiation, 81. Classic word not in the Scriptures, 82. Worst and best examples, 82. Suffering, right or wrong, the main thing in expiation, 83. Demoralizing effect of expiation, 85. It is evil paid, for evil due, 86. No instance in Scripture, 87. And no indications for it, 87. No interest of character in expiation, 90.

CHAPTER II.—LAW AND COMMANDMENT........................93
The satisfaction of law, 94. Theologic devices for this purposes, 95.

I.

Christ and his commandments, 97. Who is he to assume such a right, 98. General statement, 99. Two words, Law and Commandment, 100. What Law is, 101. What Commandment, 103. Commandment in a sense unlegal, 104. Liberty in these, 105. Christ's own exposition of them, 106. Offices and uses, 107. Law first stage of discussion, 108. No perfect institute in itself, 109. Mostly negative, 109. Has no inspirations for duty, 110. Commandment includes more and better, 111, 112. Leave the tabulated rule and embrace the divine person for law, 113. Commandment offered to faith, 114. How the two are related, 115. One a factor in nature, the other in the supernatural, 117. Law never to be taken away by redemption, 118.

II.

Great Analogies also to be noted, 120. Mother and child, 121. The school, 123. Labor and the curse, 124. The army discipline, 125. The civil state, 127. The two factor method in all these analogies, 130. No compensations here in deliverance from the law, 131. It never works destructively, 132.

III.

The gospel a twofold way of discipline in like manner, 133. GENERAL PROPOSITION to include all, 134. The penally coercive discipline, 134. No judicial penalty here, 136. The two factors work together, not one against the other, 137. No justice comes till after the discipline is through, 139. But we are kept in due impression of its future,

140. Apprehended loss of justice, 141. No thought of saving justice by penal compensations. 143. Public and Retributive justice, 145. Christ incarnated into the discipline, 147. His incarnation is the necessity of suffering accepted, 149. More to him than to us, for we do not much realize our own, 151. See no law of desert and therefore make light of it, 152. Make no sufficient account of the suffering of the good, 153. Christ's suffering great because of his purity. 154. Also by his great amount of mind. 155. Suffers in a failing cause. 157. The temptation, 158. Weeping over the city, and the agony, 159. No justice in the suffering of the cross, 161.

IV.

Some of the texts supposed to show God's dealing with Christ on the score of justice, 162. How we make proof texts, 163. No literal language for religious ideas, 163. Gratitude exaggerates always, 164. Christ made a curse, 166. Bare our sins, 167. Gives himself a ransom, 168. The scape-goat forms, 168. Forms of fifty-third of Isaiah, 169. How the commandment keeps the law, gives it back its honor, and works conjunctively with it, 173–6.

CHAPTER III.—JUSTIFICATION BY FAITH 177
Rom. iii, 25–6, How understood, 177. Two sets of words in English to represent one in the Greek, 178. Probably no relief, and can only take our disadvantage as it is, 181. Legal justification impossible, 183. Legal justification implies justification before faith, 184. The fiction supposed, 185. Also another fiction, 186. Legal satisfaction an ignoble gift for character, 187. Highest of all words for character is *right* or *righteousness*. 190.

I.

Plato and Socrates in quest of its secret power, 192. Psychological non-discovery, 193. Abraham in advance of Socrates, 194. God early declared to be source of all righteousness in men. 196. Christ puts us to the seeking after righteousness—even that of God. 197. How Christ advances the scope of the idea, 199. Legal justification cold and insufficient, 201. True justification the normal state of all created mind, 202. Faith how related to justification. 204. What the true faith is, 205. Luther's great discovery true, 206. Only his head mistook the meaning of his heart, 207. Justification and sanctification not confounded, 210.

II.

How related to imputation, 212. We are also to have our righteousness putatively in God.

CHAPTER IV.—THREEFOLD DOCTRINE OF CHRIST CONCERNING HIMSELF..218

How often has it been wished that Christ had given us a doctrine concerning himself, 218. He has done it, 218–19. His three Articles, 219. Our English word Comforter a great mistake, 220. Dispenses comfort, of course, much as Christ himself does, 222. We have missed the meaning here by not observing that the Spirit is to work in and by Christ's work, 224.

ARTICLE I.

Of sin because they believe not on me, 225. New sensibility of sin expected, 225. Defect of the old methods, 227. They did not produce the sense of sin as a state, 228. Christ reproves of sin by the sense of what is not done, 229.

ARTICLE II.

Of righteousness, because I go to the Father and ye see me no more, 230. Great and upright characters commonly not valued till they die, 231. Christ expects a great revision to occur after he is gone, 233. By what he calls righteousness he means justification, 234. And there is no legal justification possible to be thought of here, 235.

ARTICLE III.

Of judgment, because the prince of this world is judged, 236. Conceives evil to be a great organizer, 237. But the bad kingdom will be shaken by the trial scene at hand, 239. Judas, Peter, Annas, Caiaphas, all shaken, 240. Pilate himself is judged, 241. So dispossessed that he makes court to Herod, 244. All the multitude dispossessed by what they have seen, 247. All this by no display of force but only by goodness, 247.

The uses proposed to be made of this doctrine of Christ, 249. Not to be a rival doctrine, 250. To be a duplicate view that will take us away from so many literalities, 252. In the three articles we have the full scope of a gospel, 253.

Supplementary Notes, 257.

INTRODUCTION.

It seems to be required of me, by the unexpected arrival of fresh light, that I should make a large revision of my former treatise, entitled *The Vicarious Sacrifice*, and especially of the Parts III. and IV. of the same. Having undertaken to find the truth on this great subject at whatever cost, I am not willing to be excused from farther obligation because the truth appears to be outgrowing my published expositions. My former discussion has been as favorably received as I had any right to expect, and there is no reason, personal to myself, why I should be fastened to my own small measures, when larger measures are given me. Besides, how shall a man ever get rid of his old sins, when he can not let go his little outgrown opinions? Wishing no change, I have yet not ceased to consider and reconsider the whole question, as carefully as if I had not written, watching for all inward monitions and outward suggestions, whereby I might be corrected and guided farther in, to apprehend the matter of it more worthily, and in closer accord with the truth.

Since it so often helps the interest and also the understanding of the reader to know in what manner the writer came into the arguments and opinions he is trying to set forth, I feel constrained to indulge a little harmless egotism.

Thus it has happened to me twice over, when writing on two simply practical subjects, to be overtaken by surprise in suggestions setting me back on the last half of my book, and requiring amendments in it that amounted to a virtual substitution of it by new matter. I do not pretend to say that I have these amendments by any private revelation, I only know that I have them as being found by them, and not as having found them myself. Perhaps our new seeing in such matters is, at times, but our mood; and yet perhaps our mood may be our gift of seeing.

Thus, I was writing a discourse on the inquiry, How shall a man be able to entirely and perfectly forgive his enemy, so as to forever sweeten the bitterness of his wounded feeling and leave no sense of personal revulsion? I can not give the whole argument here, but it must suffice to say, that I was brought squarely down upon the discovery, that nothing will ever accomplish the proposed real and true forgiveness, but to make cost in the endeavor, such cost as new-tempers and liquefies the reluctant nature. And this making cost will be his propitiation of himself. Why not say this of all moral natures, why not of the Great Propitiation itself? Here opens my Chapter I., entitled *Forgiveness and Propitiation*.

Before the complete writing out of this, I was overtaken again by corrective suggestion at another point. Falling on the injunction by which Christ lays it on us to "keep his commandments," the prosy dullness in which we commonly embalm his words, when we draw them out as tests and lessons of practice, was forever exploded by the question occurrent, Why his commandments? Where is the law? Does he undertake to overtop Sinai, and be a new standard of character? Thus I had the Greek words *nomos* and *entolē*, before me, and they began to freshen each other in the individualities of their uses and meanings. One thought opened into another, and I began to sketch a series of articles for the press that should give a practically fresh exposition of the Saviour's word. Suffice it to say that I shortly came upon the discovery that the law-state has everywhere a commandment-state going with it, to be its consummation or crown; its fulfillment, and so, in a very important and true sense, its satisfactional substitute. Here then begins another, partly very simple, partly very subtle range of inquiry, treated of in Chapter II., called Law and Commandment. In this certain terms of our atonement language get a qualified permission, but nothing that offends the principles of right.

These two chapters, I. and II., cover the general ground of my revision, as they also do the general field of what has been called in orthodox circles the atonement; discovering, at least, the rational possibility and fact of a propitiation of God, and also a fulfillment of law by sacrifice and suffering, which, if it is not given as in penal satisfaction by the substitution of Christ, is the consummated fruit of his incarnate obedience; and since the sacrifice God makes to recover his enemies, by the death of his Son, supposes so great cost, the power it may be expected to have on human feeling and character will be rather enhanced than diminished by the correction now made. My chapter IV. occupies a ground by itself. How it came it will not be difficult to see, since it is the doctrine of Christ by Christ himself; an operative doctrine indeed, and not a formulating, giving the outfit of the Spirit and the implemental forces by which he is to work. And again, let it be the more valuable to us that it comes in after the formulating history is done, to be a gospel by Christ's own authority, not inwoven with any of the old textures of the schools, but set in by an intercalation, to have its own footing, and its regulative sway in the respectful deference of the ages to come.

It will be observed in these preliminaries that the corrections I am proposing to make do not include a return to any of the standard theologic formulas I have heretofore rejected. I recant no one of my denials. I only undertake to fill the vacant spaces made by them with better material. Thus, if any one should imagine that in now asserting the positive fact of a propitiation of God, I return to the common orthodox position, that will depend entirely upon the manner in which the propitiation is believed to be made, whether as by a legal satisfaction for sin, or wholly one side of law by a transaction in and of the divine feeling itself. I asserted a propitiation before, but accounted for the word as one by which the disciple objectivizes his own feelings, conceiving that God himself is representatively mitigated or become propitious, because he is himself inwardly reconciled to God. Instead of this, I now assert a real propitiation of God, finding it in evidence from the propitiation we instinctively make ourselves, when we heartily forgive. So if it should be imagined that I now give in to the legal-substitution, legal-satisfaction theory, it will only be true that I assert a scheme of discipline for man, which is contrived to work its own settlement, in being fulfilled and consummated by an obedience in the higher plane of liberty itself.

I still assert the "moral view" of the atonement as before, and even more completely than before; inasmuch as I propose to interpret all that is prepared and suffered in the propitiation of God and the justification of men, by a reference to the moral pronouncements of human nature and society; assuming that nothing can be true of God, or of Christ, which is not true in some sense *more humano*, and is not made intelligible by human analogies. We can not interpret God, as any one may see, except by what we find in our own personal instincts and ideas. And just here is the sin of all our theologic endeavor in the past ages, especially as regards this particular subject, that we invent so many ingredients that are verbals only, having no reality and no assignable meaning. We contrive a justice in God, which accepts the pains of innocence in place of the pains of wrong, and which is, in fact, the very essence of injustice. We contrive a forgiveness on the score of compensation, which to our human conceptions mocks the idea. We imagine that Christ has a virtue more transcendent than any of mortal kind, because it is optional; whereas nothing is a virtue save as it is done for the right, and as being under moral obligation. We conceive that Christ is even over-good in this way, better than he need be, and that the surplus he gains is a *meritum* prepared for us; asserting how often that we are saved by the merits of Christ, when we can not so much as conceive the idea. We contrive how law may be satisfied for transgressors without their punishment, and then we teach that God may justly punish after satisfaction. Our precise difficulty is, in all such impossibles of thought, that we are trying to construct the ways of God, or of his Son, without any light from our own moral instincts and ideas; to make him intelligible in the matter of a gospel, without intelligibles anywhere given to be his interpreters. We put the bits of glass and crockery into our kaleidescope, and turning it round and round we make theologic figures that we call truths, and which having no ideas in them, we think must surely stand, because they look so regular and are milled in the scientific way of the scientific instrument. Thus we go on from age to age, trying vainly to fasten theologic notions that represent God by nothing in ourselves. Is it not time now, after so many centuries gone by, to have it discovered, that there is no truth concerning God which is not somehow explicated by truths of our own moral consciousness?

If now these prefatory specifications signify less, taken by themselves, than might be desired, they will at least have a certain value in suggesting beforehand what I myself conceive to be the significance or intended amount of the reconstructions offered—that I do not undertake to be orthodox, but to be more sufficiently and scripturally true.

It will be understood, I presume, that I suppose the two revised statements, or solutions of doctrine I am now going to propound, to be really new. I frankly allow that I do, and also as frankly confess that in this simple fact my courage and confidence are most weakened by misgivings. For who can expect a great subject like this, which has engaged so many of the most gigantic minds of so many past ages, to be now, in these last times, more sufficiently apprehended and better expounded by an ordinary teacher, at his common level of standing. It is difficult, I allow, not to be greatly appalled when confronted by this objection. But it must not be forgotten that now and then some person will be stronger in his accidents, than other and greater men have been in their powers; also that God himself sometimes makes accidents for mind by his own private touch, when he will unfold some needed lesson; also that God has a way of preparing times for the uncovering of truth, and that as he would not have his Son appear till the fullness of time should come, so he will not expect his Son's gospel to be duly conceived till the times are ready and all the suggestive conditions ripe that may set us in upon it. No greatest man or champion is going to conquer a truth before its time, and no least competent man, we may also dare to say, need miss of a truth when its time has come, and the flags of right suggestion are all out before him. How easy a thing it is, in fact, to think what the times have got ready to be thought, and are even whispering to us from behind all curtains of discovery, and out of all most secret nooks and chambers of experience. That now the clock has finally struck, and the day has fully come for some new and different thinking of this great subject, I most verily believe. And, to make this evident, I propose to occupy the few remaining pages of this preliminary chapter in showing by what signs the two staple matters of what has heretofore been called the Christian Atonement, viz., Propitiation and Legal Substitution, appear to be asking, or rather expectantly waiting, for some more satisfactory, better grounded exposition.

In the original word of Scripture the truths revealed are either visibly or verbally presented from that other side of heavenly announcement whence they come. There is no sympathy as yet, no twofold thinking in the forms, for they represent one party only. But the supposition is, that being given to intelligence, intelligence will fall at work upon them, and that human thought, laboring in the outward images of things, will generate modes of speech and laws of experience that compose a kind of second language on the base-level of nature. And so it will, by and by, begin to be the problem how to get the simple indicative matter of revelation into the forms of thought prepared in the thought-language of the mere understanding. The problem is, to accomplish a marriage of the two parties, and get the declarative work grafted in upon the natural analogies, when it will be so much closer to the common life of men, and settle its hold just so much more firmly on their convictions. We must not be so jealous of naturalism as to be alarmed by this process. It is not the supernatural submitting itself to nature to be buried and lost, but going down to hook itself in upon nature by seizing on the analogies of thought and law; so to become fast locked in all the terms of experience and opinion which thought has generated. The bent we are thus receiving more and more distinctly towards nature and science is not wholly mischievous, as many appear to assume in their nervous dread of naturalism, but is our instinctive endeavor to obtain a new anchorage ground for christian truths and ideas, where they will hold us more firmly, and yield us a more settled confidence. To change the figure, we digest the declarative matter supernaturally given, and turn it into chyle for the absorbent action of our intelligence, in the plane of life where we grow our common thought and frame our common judgments.

Thus our fathers, down to a few generations back, made up their account of human depravity under what they called "the covenant of works;" and only could not be sure, whether the propagation of it was "by the federal headship established in that covenant," or "by Adam sinning for us," or "by our own sinning in Adam," or by "God putting over Adam's sin upon us by an act of imputation." All which is substituted now, with how great advantage, by simply conceiving that every sinning man is retributively damaged in his person by the effect of his sin, which damage is propagated of necessity in his posterity, by well known laws of physiology.

In the same way all the expectances of christian nurture were set forth, and conceived to have their pledge in "the covenant of Abraham," and laborious argumentations were drawn out to show that the sacrament of baptism followed the sacrament of circumcision, connecting us back, as it were across the sea, with that far off, dimly beheld dispensation of promise. Whereas now we behold a promise always at hand in the laws of physiology, finding how, in their dispensation, every good element and gracious longing works reproductively in the child, to fashion, as by a law, the lineaments of a divine life established in its parent. And then, furthermore, after the child is born, we do not see it to be a wholly separate creature at first, but regard it for a long time still as being in the matrix of a parental culture, where it is wax to every temper, feeling, sentiment, all that bathes it in expression, all that is done for it and round it. And then to finish out our conception, instead of going back to Abraham, to imagine some blessing coming out of Abraham's faith, we say, without scruple, that we mean to have our child "grow up" in the faith.

We get a similar advantage when we put ourselves to the question of Christ's divinity. Piling on scripture citations ought to sufficiently prove it. And yet after it is proved in this manner, it will scarcely seem to be true. There is, in fact, no way to make out his divinity, so effective and true as to put him down into humanity, under the laws of humanity, and see, from his childhood onward, whether he stays there. Starting him above the level of humanity, there to simply continue and be, embalmed in texts, makes him a kind of riddle in his story—we can no way master it, and are sure of nothing concerning it—but when we find that we can not keep him under manhood after we have put him there, he will have proved his divinity by experiment. The Unitarians have been of great service to us here; for when we start with them, at their point of born humanity, we find him shooting proudly up out of human range and level, in all the wonders of his great life and character, and by no fit name can we call him but Immanuel. The closer we bring him down to manhood the more evidently, visibly, indisputably superhuman, or divine he appears.

In the same way again we have found our advantage in a less ghostly way of conceiving the supernatural. We tried a long time, and some are trying still, to think it as a phantasmagoric affair that is *super* as regards nature, and comes out apparition-wise in prodigies and flitting visitations, supernaturally disturbing our mortal affairs. Therefore believing, it may be, in supernaturals that occurred a long time ago, or clear back in the beginnings of revelation, we took up the impression that such things were credible when they were far enough off; but that any thing so irregular may be occurring now, we assumed to be wholly incredible. What then is nature, we have lately begun to ask, as related to the supernatural? and what is the supernatural as related to nature? And one, we learn to say, is the world under causes, the other the world above causes. One is matter and force, the other is mind in the self-arbitrament of will. Whereupon it is discovered, strange to say, that we act supernaturally ourselves, and are in fact supernatural beings. All minds, in all orders and worlds, created and uncreated, make up thus a realm supernatural, under whose action nature is every where flexible as a hand for its uses. And the supernatural is only just as much more real than nature as it is more sovereign, and more nearly universal. We get a place for it thus, where it shows itself as a factor in our common life, and as such is the subject of our consciousness. We no longer perambulate the sky and climb over the moon to find it, but we have it as a fact familiar to our knowledge.

Again, we get a solid footing in the same manner for the great gospel fact of vicarious sacrifice, by showing its correspondence and symbolic natural agreement with facts and demonstrations occurring all the while in our human relations. All love, as we perceive, reveals the vicarious instinct, either natural or religious. The sad story of a child in the street, the moan of a wounded stranger by the roadside, engages it. The malefactor dying for his crime will none the less burden some good man's heart, but possibly the more, that he suffers only what he deserves. And so the mother, the friend, the patriot, are all specially charged with their own special burden of concern or sorrow. Half the wants that gird our industry, and half the cost we undergo in our feeling, are instigated by our vicarious relations and offices. And Christ is with us under like instigations, only immeasurably above us in the scope of his sympathies and the generally perfect fullness of his aims and dispositions. Nothing is easier to believe than that he, in this most humanly natural and worthy sense, bows himself to suffering in a mission of vicarious sacrifice. But if, taking hold of certain highly figurative phraseologies, we conceive them prosily enough to convert the matter of the vicarious suffering into penal endurances under the justice of God, we recoil from believing a story of supernatural goodness so doubtfully good. Even if we say that we believe, our faith is choked by a jealousy of mistake, and we are scarce able to hold ourselves to any but a very thin, misgiving sort of confidence.

Edwards drew what I look upon as the finest paragraph in all his works, setting forth Christ in the sentiment of his vicarious relation to men as their Redeemer and Saviour. And yet he could not imagine that it amounted to very much more than a pleasant commendation of him to our human feeling. That it showed the very essence of the substitution—how " he bore our sins in his own body on the tree," how "God laid on him the iniquity of us all," and how " the chastisement of our peace was upon him "—he did not so much as imagine; that was something more literal, and not to be explained by any such mere human analogies. " Christ's great love," he says, "and pity to the elect was one source of his suffering—[one source only]. A strong exercise of pity excites a lively idea of the misery under which he pities them, * * his love and pity fixed the idea of them in his mind as if he had really been they, and fixed their calamity in his mind as though it had been really his. A very strong and lively love and pity towards the miserable, tends to make their case ours; as in other respects so in this, in particular, as it doth in our idea place us in their stead, under their misery, with a most lively feeling sense of that misery, as it were feeling it for them, actually suffering it in their stead by strong sympathy."* And yet he could not see the atonement here; that was transacted on the nails and the wood! As if the mere suffering of his human body were any thing in comparison with the great moral woe of his heart, or as if it were intended to be any thing but an outward sign of that. We see from his words that he had the key in his hand, but he did not dare to use

---

* *Miscellaneous observations.*

it. Had he thus been able to see the matter of the sacrifice in the moral analogies so powerfully sketched by himself, instead of lapsing under the jargon of penalties endured and legal compensations paid to justice, what strength and clearness would he have added to all our christian ideas—giving us a gospel simple as our own human feeling, and faithfully interpreted and verified by it.

It only remains to add, in this connection, that what I am now proposing, in my chapters on the Propitiation, and Law and Commandment, is to bring these points away from the wrangle in which they are held, and show them as given to intelligence, under the same great analogies where the other christian truths referred to are beginning to be received and rested in with such increase of confidence.

Let me now proceed to add some reasons why a specially deliberate attention to this subject of penal atonement appears to be demanded at the present time; and if possible some revision of doctrine that will arm us against the incoming perils. For it is not any longer to be disguised that a time of jeopardy has come, and jeopardy revealed, we are not to forget, is God's last impulse of discovery for truths the groping ages have missed. A certain general momentum of thought is becoming every day more and more pressingly adverse on this particular side of what we call our gospel. It rolls in with a steady, sea-surge motion, piling tides that even threaten to overtop and completely drown out the so called orthodox belief. It is not that Unitarian arguments, maintained by Unitarians themselves, are at all more impressive than they have been, but that there is a growing multitude in our own churches, and a still larger more heavily insurgent multitude outside, who, in tones that indicate all kinds of tempers, gentle and fierce, candid and contemptuous, join their testimony against all that we have been calling Expiation and Legal Atonement. Apologies to save and refortify the ground we are losing, even bear a look of exhausted iteration that weakens belief. And what can even new argument do, if any such is possible, in upholding, as for God, terms of proceeding, miscalled ways of grace, which it is getting to be generally agreed would forever dishonor a man dealing with his fellow. The condemning voices, we have long seen, are increasing in number, and their confidence is more emboldened by their better command of their subject. The press is theirs, and they almost take possession of the current literature. On what point the movement is advancing, and with what results to come, it is not difficult to see; and a great many of the truest and best disciples are quite distressed by what looks to them like a day at hand of general overthrow. Is it not possible for them to believe that confidence and hope are still permitted? Let them see and be sure that all which their faith stands by is to stand, and that only the unwisdoms of men are to vanish away.

Another consideration must not be omitted; viz., that our modern undertaking of gospel missions abroad requires of us a thorough reinvestigation, and, if necessary, a faithful reconstruction of our doctrine; that we may have it intermixed with no needless offenses, and loaded with no artificial impediments. We can not convert the world with an outfit which is lumber and not armor. Subordinate truths will of course have a subordinate consequence, but the great central truth of the Redemption misconceived, or only half conceived, or mixed with conceptions that are morally revolting, will but stumble on its way, and, even if it wins a sort of victory, will come to its end in disastrous overthrow. It is unpleasant to be afflicted with misgivings of this kind in a work so grandly beneficent and so closely bound up with the love of God, but it is not easy to be entirely clear of them. By our missions we are now put face to face with the whole eastern half population of the globe. Is there no reason to fear that we have precipitated ourselves upon them without a sufficient understanding either of their religious position or their intellectual capacity; or what is more to be regretted, without any such preparation of doctrine as would help us to effectually pour in the love of God on their subtle refinements and the congeries of theosophic delusions they maintain as religions? After twelve or twenty years of missionary life among them, Dr. Duff revisited Scotland, and published his heavy octavo volume on their religious faith and condition. Not long after his return to his field he discovered, just what some of us suspected in reading his book, that he had missed the point of insight, and that back of the coarse and revolting superstitions he had looked upon as their religion, they had rich stores of learning and philosophy, including much valuable truth. I have not seen the retraction he published, but only the report of it; suffice it to say that no such misconceptions are any longer possible; for we know as a matter of common intelligence that these people have their bodies of literature reaching back to the earliest ages of human story; scholars of great culture practiced in the subtlest refinements of speculation; tenets and maxims of conduct not seldom worthy of christianity itself.

Now that such peoples, however much impressed with our superiority in arms and naval arts, in constitutional law and liberty, and above all in material wealth and production, are going to have the faith of a gospel suddenly precipitated on them, and become christians by simple notification, is a most irrational confidence. Our first thing is to be sure for ourselves that the christianity we offer them is the true, cumbered by no revolting speculations, disfigured by no jargon of false theory; and then that we so far understand their religious prepossessions and prejudices that we can make our christian approach by fit adaptations, and engage their assent by a thoroughly appreciative judgment of their truths and errors. They are warming now to a glow, we hear, in their own cause, which is proof, beyond a question, that our christianity will gain them only by the mastering of their strength, and not by any dictation put upon their weakness. As many as eighty newspapers, we are told, have sprung into circulation in the native languages of India within a very few years. They are almost all in the interest of political democracy. Many of them too are discussing the question whether christianity has any claim to being accepted as the universal religion, some of them boldly insisting on its inferiority to the faith of Buddha or Lao-tse, and stating their critical reasons. Chunder Sun, meantime, is pushing out through India in his campaign of reform, to new organize the old religion; having already gathered his sixty-five circles, or institutes of worship, designing to establish a great enduring religion on the roots of the Indian history. We also hear that the government University for English culture at Bombay, matriculating year by year its eight hundred students, shows them falling off into a general contempt of Christianity; and our missionaries, unable to cope with so great unbelief, send over to engage one of our ablest and most eloquent professors in a course of lectures for their benefit. Doubtless he has done all that could be done in that manner, but what can any so casual, or merely occasional effort do for the rooting of a faith that has no roots, and scarcely a soil to feed them? We are also told by Mr. Nevius, in his late interesting book, how the students of Shantung University in China carry on their debates with christianity. They object to the trinity as impossible; also to the incarnation, or to the new personality it produces, for like reasons. Then also they ask why christianity so constantly "appeals to motives resting upon the doctrine of future rewards and punishments, instead of taking the higher ground of urging men to the practice of virtue, simply because it is right and obligatory?" And then again, "Is it consistent with the justice of God to punish the innocent and clear the guilty, as he does in visiting the penalty of death on the Saviour, and letting the sinner go free?" The three objections first named are intellectual, and may probably be well enough removed by a skillful statement, but the last is moral, and never was, or can be, so stated as to take away the offense it creates. And how many times have our missionaries reported this objection made by the malignants of unbelief, regarding it, of course, as so much evidence given of their reprobate condition! A very sad thing it is that good men can be dealing out offense for gospel in this manner, and expecting men to be saved by what only shocks the most original and best convictions of their moral nature. Is it not a matter of supreme consequence in this view, as regards our missionary engagements, that we find how to drop out of Christ's reconciling work what the Scripture does not teach, save in figurative expressions never meant to be understood as they have been, and put the truth of it in such harmony with the supreme beauty and perfectness of God as will never shock or repel, but only draw men to its loving embrace. I certainly think it can be done, even as Christ himself assumed, when he said, "I will draw all men unto me."

Once more, as we are encountering a new age of doubt that disallows the faith of any thing supernatural, and as the gospel itself is crowded closer to the wall than ever before, because of its intensely supernatural character, we can not afford to hold on upon any sort of incumbrance that weakens our doctrine or makes it incredible. It must be enough that we maintain our ground in what are called offenses against reason, without having it put upon us to maintain offenses against immutable morality. "Laying aside every weight" is even divine counsel for us now, and requires us to be stripping here for the freest encounter possible. We must not be hampered longer by volunteer wisdoms that choke our breath and stifle our confidence.

According to our new gospel of naturalism, there is nothing to be done for souls in the preparation of character, save by educating, or evolving, or developing, what is in them. Development is the word most common, and it even begins to be a staple word in sermons; the conception being that there are stock powers on hand that have only to be run, or operated under their own natural laws, to develop some time or other all the graces of a completely finished virtue. At present, or in this first stage, they do not show all that can be desired, being under misdirecting circumstance, or cause, or tempestuous appetite or passion. We used to call it sin, but the simple fact is, it is now discovered, that we are doing just as we were made to do, and are on the way to get by our misdirections and come out fully ripe in good. If we commit murder, it is not wholesome; if we lie, our lie so called is weak, but is in the way to come out just as good as the truth. And so we find a sovereign gospel in development that works by nature, no thanks to supernatural grace, or help from any quarter. We are kept thus in the integrity of reason, it is said. We do not want, or believe, any miracle, or any supernatural person, or in fact any salvation; all such incredibles we reject before argument.

Our christian gospel meantime begins at the grand first point of depravity and moral incapacity, so finely and with such evident truth asserted by Plato. Thus, after showing that men are good "neither by nature nor by instruction," he answers the question How? *"This I think could not be shown easily, but I conjecture that the property of goodness is something specially divine, and that good men exist as prophets do and oracle chanters. For these exist neither by nature nor by art, but become such by the inspiration of the gods." What height of possibility for man is this, to be inwoven thus with God-help and quickened by the perfect life of God! If then some are willing to believe that man is a mere animal, grown up to his present pitch of capacity by the processes of natural selection, what loss of dignity will they look for instead, when, by a selection reaching downward, he forswears affinity with God? What hope is there for man, asks Plato, but in God's inspirations? Therefore Christ appears—the Grand Chief Miracle of the world—doing every thing he does in human life by miracle, if only it were done with outward show to keep the wonders manifest. He comes to quicken life where it is gone out. He proposes a new birth, and a passing thereby from death to life. He undertakes more than to be the power of a new development, to be himself the new grain planted for de-

---

* Dialogue on Virtue.

velopment. He propounds his mission as the mission of a Saviour come to bring salvation. He counts on no stock powers in human nature that are going to mend themselves; nothing short of a salvation brought down from out of nature and above, in his divine person, can be any sufficient remedy. This most certainly is what is given us for gospel, and this we are firmly to hold and boldly publish. I for one believe in it with all my heart. And if I can not have it to believe in, I want no other, more daintily or less ruggedly and squarely pronounced. All the better right have we therefore to insist that, while we are asserting faithfully this supernatural salvation—less popular than it was, attacked more frequently by argument, and ready, as some think, to be quite gone by—we be not also obliged to maintain doctrines of the salvation which are themselves an offense to right sentiment and the sturdiest inborn principles of our moral nature itself.

Proposing then, as I do here, a conception of *Propitiation* and of *Law and Commandment*, that clears all such incumbrance, I think my argument is entitled, in advance, to greater favor and consideration, than it ever could have been in any former age of the world. For the time has now come, as never before, when the gospel can not afford to work at disadvantage and carry weights that do not belong to it.

FORGIVENESS AND LAW.

CHAPTER I.

FORGIVENESS AND PROPITIATION, WITHOUT EXPIATION.

The argument of my former treatise was concerned in exhibiting the work of Christ as a reconciling power on men. This was conceived to be the whole import and effect of it; just as, in our current theology, it is conceived to be a work that reconciles God—sometimes a propitiation, such as mitigates or conciliates the dispositions of God in the forgiveness of sins; and sometimes, with far less appearance of possibility, an expiation that satisfies the justice of God, and allows him to yield the forgiveness legally.

I now propose to substitute, for the latter half of my former treatise, a different ex- *Proposed revision.* position; composing thus a whole of doctrine that comprises both the reconciliation of men to God, and of God to men. I have still as little question now as before, that the main significance of the gospel is in what it does, or undertakes to do, for the reconciliation of men. Indeed, a great part of the texts cited for atonement, so called, conceiving it as a conciliation of God, have their whole meaning, if rightly understood, at the other pole of the subject. And nothing is now so much wanted, to set the gospel in its true proportion, as a just reclamation of these texts in the meaning they have lost.

When we speak, as I am now to speak, of the propitiation of God, having it as our assumed undertaking to show the fact of such a propitiation antecedently related to the forgiveness of sins, we seem to be thrusting ourselves on a matter high above our reach, and in its own nature altogether improbable. There is even a look of offense and mortal presumption in the proposal itself. I am also pressed with the conviction that my single arguments first named will seem inconclusive, or even weak; for there is no determinate position here to be taken that will turn the question logically by itself. I have never handled a subject where all the parts and complexities of evidence are so necessary to be had in sight together, in order to any just impression. In this view, let me ask of my reader to go quite through my chapter, and get all my points in view, before he begins to set his opinions adversely in finalities of judgment passed before the time.

There is, it is true, one great principle or funda-
The one sovereign principle. mental fact which runs through the whole subject as presented, and is, in a sense, the universal solvent of it, but that will not be seen at any single glance, and can not bring God into the range of a probable partakership with us, in the necessities of propitiation, till it has been long enough canvassed to reveal what is in it. The fact

of which I speak is the grand analogy, or almost identity that subsists between our moral nature and that of God; so that our moral pathologies and those of God make faithful answer to each other, and he is brought so close to us that almost any thing that occurs in the workings or exigencies of our moral instincts may even be expected in his.

It has been a question whether to begin this discussion at the scripture texts, in which propitiation is asserted—as I formerly thought it was not, save in a certain objective way of accommodation—but as the view I am to advance opened first at the question of forgiveness by men toward men, I will start my argument from that point, and bring in the scripture proofs farther on, where they will have some complexions of thought prepared to soften their incredibility.

Begin at forgiveness.

I.

In the New Testament it will be observed that forgiveness by God and forgiveness by men are set forth mutually, one by the help of the other. "Forgiving one another, even as God for Christ's sake [ἐν Χριστῷ] hath forgiven you." "Forgive us our trespasses as we forgive them that trespass against us." One kind of forgiveness matches and interprets the other; for they have a common property. They come to the same point when they are genuine, and require also exactly the same preparations and conditions precedent. It

Forgiveness by God and men the same.

is not commonly supposed, I know, that forgiveness by men requires any thing done which is in the nature of propitiation. But we had best make nothing of that; for, in fact, the matter of forgiveness by men is so indeterminately thought, or so nearly unattempted by analysis, that we really do not know what is in it, or how it comes, or what it does. We talk of it in a certain loose way, but have really no moral casuistry by which we regulate our practice in it.

What then do we mean by forgiveness when we speak of forgiving an enemy or wrong doer?—what, that is, by a man's forgiveness of a man? I suppose that a great many persons never had a thought of it as signifying more than the mere passing of the word. They even choke at this, and only stammer it in under-tone when it is passed. As if the mere getting out of the word "I forgive" were the consummation of their duty-struggle in the question.

Nothing is more evident, to any one who cares to understand what is to be done in such a matter, than that the mere passing of the word *forgive* constitutes no new relation. It may be that the forgiving party only says it, just to be quit of his adversary. He does it as a mere letting go, or waiving of the man, not as a true taking hold of him rather for eternal brotherhood's sake. He is only thinking quite commonly, in this letting go, how to be let go himself, and have his obligation ended. Sometimes it will be even thought, if not spoken aloud, "Yes, I forgive him, but I hope never to see him

Not negative.

again." Or it will be said, "Yes, I forgive, but I can never forget." Or, again, "Yes, and I do not much care whether he repents of his wrong or not, if only I can be quit of all connection with him." I can not specify, and need not, all the loose ways and turns of mock sentiment, by which this grace of forgiveness is corrupted and made to be no grace at all, but only a plausible indifference under the guises of grace. It is how often but a kind of hypocrisy under which the forgiving man is hidden from his own discovery.

All this in a way of transition; the cases referred to are only cases where irresponsible, self-serving, worldly men, whether nominally christian or not, cheapen the duty of forgiveness by light performance, or slip it by evasions and tricks of words. But there are troubles of mind in respect to this matter of forgiveness that are real, *The difficulty real.* and are encountered by the best and holiest men. They mean to be forgiving, and live in the habit of it universally. Is it not the love of God that they have accepted as their ruling principle and joy—love, that is, to every body, including even their enemies? Yes, but the love of God prepares not even him to forgive by itself, as we shall by and by see. Not more certainly will it prepare any best and most loving of mankind to forgive. We take up certain modes of speaking which imply that love is a kind of total virtue, and will carry all other graces and virtues with it. And it will, in the sense of causation, or of being their causative spring. But it does not

4

follow that it will dispense forgivenesses without also preparing the necessary antecedent propitiations. A good man lives in the unquestionable sway of universal love to his kind. If then one of them does him a bitter injury, will he therefore launch an absolute forgiveness on him? If he were nothing but love—if he were no complete moral nature—he might. But he is a complete moral nature, having other involuntary sentiments that come into play along-side of love, and partly for its sake—the sense of being hurt by wrong, indignations against wrong done to others, disgusts to what is loathsome, contempt of lies, hatred of oppression, anger hot against cruel inhumanities—all these animosities, or revulsions of feeling, fasten their grip on the malefactor sins and refuse to let go. And they do it as for society and the law-state of discipline; composing a court of arbitrament that we call moral opinion, which keeps all wrong doing and wrong doers under sanctions of public opprobrium and silent condemnation. Filling an office so important, they must not be extirpated under any pretext of forgiveness.* They require to be somehow mastered, and somehow to remain. And the supreme art of forgiveness will consist in finding how to embrace the unworthy as if they were not unworthy, or how to have them still on hand when they will not suffer the forgiveness to pass. Which supreme art is the way of propitiation—always concerned in the reconciliation of moral natures separated by injuries.

---

* Note 1.

How it is that the forgivenesses of good men so often miscarry, will be sufficiently explained by the exposition here given. It does not follow that they are to be impeached for obstinacy or insincerity. They meant to forgive and make clean work of their forgiveness. But their old mind returns upon them and their old animosities are rekindled, as if only banked in their fires and not extinguished. They look on the faces and hear the voices of the men they undertook to forgive, and their disgusts come back on them. The old words rattle as if in new offenses, and there is no moral gong at hand by which they can be drowned. Now the difficulty very often is that the forgiven party has never been so qualified by grace that he could fitly be forgiven. But that is no sufficient excuse; for the forgiving party can be right even if there is no forgiveness passed. In most cases the true account of the matter is that the forgiving party did not find how to be fitly propitiated, and was not qualified antecedently by such a state of preparation as his own moral nature and necessities demanded. What he so honestly meant to do, therefore, he is not unlikely mortified by and by to discover is not effectually done.

How forgivenesses fail.

True forgiveness then, that which forgives as God in Christ hath forgiven, is no such letting up simply of revenge against the wrong doer as was first described—no shove of dismission, no dumb turning of the back. Neither is it any mere setting of the will to do a deed of love, as we often discover in really good men—no drumming of the hard sentiments and revulsions and moral condemnations to sleep. Perhaps they were not meant to go to sleep, but to stay by rather in such welcome as the new cast of a right propitiation will suffer.

And in order to this, two things are necessary; first, such a sympathy with the wrong-doing party as virtually takes his nature; and secondly, a making cost in that nature by suffering, or expense, or painstaking sacrifice and labor. The sympathy must be of that positive kind which wants the man himself, and not a mere quiet relationship with him; wants him for a brother, considers nothing to be really gained till it has gained a brother. The sympathy needs to be such as amounts to virtual identification, where there is a contriving how to feel the man all through, and read him as by inward appreciation, to search out his good and evil, his weaknesses and gifts, his bad training and bad associations, his troubles and trials and wrongs—so to understand and, as it were, be the man himself; having him interpreted to the soul's love, by setting all tenderest, most exploring affinities in play, finding how to work engagement in him, and learn what may best be touched or taken hold of in a way to make him a friend. Taking the wrong doer thus upon itself, it will also take, in a certain sense, his wrong to be forgiven; for its longing is after some most real identification with the fellow nature sought after. Thus we see that, to really for-

Two things necessary.

give and make clean work of it, requires a going
through into good, if possible, with the wrong doer,
and meeting him there, both reconciled. And when
it is done thoroughly enough to configure and new-tone
the forgiving party as well as the forgiven, he is so far
become himself a reconciled or propitiated man, as
truly as the other is become a forgiven or restored
man. Or if the man so propitiated is repelled in
the forgiveness he offers, he is, humanly speaking,
but as one that came unto his own and his own received him not.

But there remains, as was just now intimated, a
second indispensable condition, by which the advances of sympathy, finding their way Making cost for
into and through wrong doers and enemies.
enemies, will become a more nearly absolute power in
them, and a more complete propitiation for them;
viz., in the making cost and bearing heavy burdens
of painstaking and sorrow to regain them and be
reconciled to them. The injured party has a most
powerful and multiform combination of alienated and
offended sentiment struggling in his nature. And,
in one view, it is right that he should have. He
could not be a proper man, least of all a holy man,
without them. His integrity is hurt, his holiness
offended, his moral taste disgusted. He is alienated, thrown off, thrust back into separation, by the
whole instinct of his moral nature. The fires of his
purity smoke. His indignations scorch his love, and
without any false fire of revenge, which is too com-

monly kindled also, he seems to himself to be in a revulsion that he has no will to subdue. He is a wounded man whose damaged nature winces even in his prayers. So that if he says "I forgive," with his utmost stress of emphasis, he will not be satisfied with any meaning he can force into the words. Is he therefore to be blamed, that he has so many of these dissentient feelings struggling in him to obstruct his forgivenesses? No, not in the sense that he has them, but only in the sense that he does not have them mitigated, or propitiated so as to be themselves in consent, or subjected by sacrifice. Let him find how to plough through the bosom of his adversary by his tenderly appreciative sympathy, how to appear as a brotherly nature at every gate of the mind, standing there as in cost, to look forgiveness without saying it, and he will find, however he may explain it or not explain it, that there is a wonderful consent in his feeling somehow, and that he is perfectly atoned [at-oned] both with himself and his adversary.

To explain this whole matter analytically I acknowledge to be difficult. Let me give it in the concrete in three or four examples. The first, which is very simple, I will give more at large that we may note in transition some of the points which are likely to occur, on the way to a complete forgiveness.

Thus you had, we may suppose, a partner in trade whom you had taken up out of his very dejected lot of poverty. Discovering talent and what you thought was character in him,

<small>A case supposed.</small>

you took him into confidence, to share your fortunes with you. Before you suspected danger from him, he had used the name and credit of your company, under cover of his legal rights, in a most faithless and cruel violation of trust, such as plucked you down out of wealth, and reduced you to a lot of poverty so nearly complete that you had not even bread for your children. But your industry and worth brought you up again finally to affluence; while the vices into which he fell brought him down to want and hopeless destitution. Meantime, in all the intervening years you have been remembering his wrong, which you could not well forget. His name has been, of course, a name significant of bitter wrong in your house, and so connected with pain as to be seldom or never spoken—a word as it were for the dumb. You have said inwardly, "I must forgive," and you have meant, on principle, to do it, perhaps really supposed it to be done; but there is, nevertheless, to this day a sting in that name, and you do not like to hear it. To meet him on the street, or catch the look of his face, pains you, and you inwardly shudder as you pass him, at the discovery that, christian man as you are, you are certainly not reconciled to him, and see not how you ever can be. But you are shortly to find how you can be. The poor man, going down under his vices, loses name and figure and is all but forgotten. But you hear that his family are suffering in bitter want. Did you not say that you could forgive, and what is come now but your opportunity? You send them in supplies and means of comfort, once and again, concealing always your name, lest it may seem to be your revenge. By and by his son is arrested for crime, and who but you will volunteer to give the needed bail? and that requires your name. At length some infectious disease falls on the forlorn being and his family, and who will peril life, in giving help and watch to people so completely out of consideration? But you said your forgiveness long ago, and what shall you do to make it good but go in to minister and be their saviour? The poor fellow turns himself to the wall when he sees you and weeps aloud, saying not a word, but just covering his face with his hands and smothering his broken-hearted shame as he best can. Where now, on your part, is the reluctance and revulsion that so often stifled your forgiveness? Gone, all gone, forever! The word itself is become the sweetest of all words. By your painstaking endeavor, and the peril you have borne for your enemy, you are so far reconciled in your own nature that you can now completely forgive, whether he can rightly be forgiven or not. He can not be till he comes into a genuinely right mind, though still you none the less truly forgive. The forgiveness in you is potentially complete, even though it should never be actually sealed upon him. You have taken his sin upon you in the cost you have borne for his sake, and what you have borne thus freely for him quells that unreducible something, that dumb ague of justice that was disallowing your forgivenesses. It is even as if there had been a great sacrifice transacted in your soul's court of sacrifice, by which your condemnations that were blocking your sensibilities have been smoothed and soothed and taken away. Under so great patience and cost, the forgiving charities are all out in your feeling, fresh and clean, and swinging the censers of their worship to pay the fragrant honors due.

Take another example, that is short and sharp, but unites all the elements, either by implication or expressly. A noted English preacher, traveling on horseback in the country, is stopped by a footpad demanding his purse. Asking, "Will you let me pray?" he immediately descends and begins a prayer. It is fervently made for both parties, and begins forthwith to be answered by a thought occurrent that contains the answer; an answer that makes heavy cost for him, and mortgages much that is most precious in life's comforts to the robber. Rising to his feet he questions how a life so unjust and wicked was begun, charges it kindly to some sorrowful defect of nurture, some atmosphere of positively bad example. Still the wrong and danger of it are none the less evident, for it is, how plainly, a life that is both against God and against society. "Come now," he says, "let me offer you something better. Go home with me and take employment in my service. I will see that no human being, not even my family, shall know of this affair as long as we live." Accepting the offer, the man took service with his benefactor, and his crime was never known till it

Another example.

was reported, in a voluntary confession from his own lips, on the day of his master's funeral. The cost made by this man of God, in taking thus an unknown robber into his family, and trusting his and their lives to his fidelity, was about as heavy as it well could be. How complete also was the resulting forgiveness, we can see from the double trust that followed; the master trusting the man, and the man the master, for so many years of trial, in a matter always secret between them.

But we have a larger field of forgivenesses, and we are always in it; and here it is even our instinct to make cost freely, in order to keep our intractable ugly nature pliant to this gentle ministry. We have much to forgive that is not done against ourselves, but against our friends and fellow disciples, against purity and truth and love, against God, and Christ, and religion. And the offenses done, in so many ways and relations, are often dreadfully revolting—cruelties to the weak, violences to the just, vices all disgust, mockeries of what is holy, insults to Christ, so that we are set burning, as it were, in a kind of divine animosity, such as the Psalmist utters in what some hastily reprobate as the scandalous zeal of passion, when he says, "I hate them with perfect hatred, I count them mine enemies." He might have been a very great fanatic in that key, but he probably was not. God himself is in offense in just that way, and ought to be; only he will have it for his merit that, being thus exas-

<small>Another.</small>

perated, he can, without self-blame, mitigate his offense and train it to forgiveness. Much easier and more natural, at least, is it for us to end off our duty to the incorrigible and wicked in our condemnations. Our drift in this direction is so strong that we sometimes let our prayers scorch heaven over them. We forget that we are to gain them and bring them into God's forgiveness and ours by making cost for them. Perhaps we are sometimes willing to have their sins make large amount of cost for them—counting this, it may be, our righteousness. No, it is a great mistake, and we really do not mean it. What we want, after all, is not to have them get their deserts, but to have them recovered to God and forgiven. And that we shall not obtain for them till we begin to bear their sin, suffer patiently their unworthiness, and work and wait in all painstaking on their insensibility; and then, when our hard way of natural condemnation is duly softened, there is at least a chance that theirs may be. No, it must not be forgotten, that beautiful word of the Master, "Whosesoever sins ye remit, they are remitted unto them." We get other men's sins remitted of God, when we are deep enough in cost to remit them ourselves. And this exactly is the secret of those times of religious fervor in communities which are so great a mystery to many. The whole christian mind has forgotten to be a judging and become a forgiving mind. And it has become a forgiving mind by the key of sacrifice and painstaking cost into which it has fallen. This, observe, is the cross, and when a community is in it, forgiveness runs full circle, and the church-state is a state of life.

Now in these three examples given for illustration, we see how it is that forgivenesses in men are ripened and fully brought to pass only as propitiations are. Also that our human instinct puts us therefore always on making cost when we undertake to really forgive. Also that human forgivenesses are possible to be consummated only by the help of some placation or atonement, or cost-making sacrifice. The forgiving party must be so far entered into the lot and state of the wrong-doing party, as to be thoroughly identified with him, even to the extent of suffering by him and for him. Some alterative must be taken by the man who will truly forgive, that has power to liquefy the indifferences, or assuage the stern, over-loaded displeasures, of his moral and morally injured, morally revolted nature. He may settle into a callous and dull state, by just staying at his point of uncaring self-content— but his callousness will be simply disendowed sensibility, and not forgiveness. If the offense he suffers from the wrong of his enemy is ever to be cleared, his forgivenesses will be drawn out only by such freedom in the matter of cost as opens the sluices of his feeling, and waters the dry rock about which his indignations are smoking. Suffering, in short, is with all moral natures, the necessary correlate of forgiveness. The man, that is, can not say "I forgive," and have the saying end it; he must somehow atone both him-

Propitiation the common exigent of life.

self and his enemy, by a painstaking, rightly so called, that has power to recast the terms of their relationship. So far from its being an absurd thing to speak of a propitiation as the necessary precondition of forgiveness, no human creature will ever keep himself reconciled to his kind, without finding how in some of its degrees to practice it. Instead of being a great theologic mystery, it is even the common exigent of life. Doubtless we may live in the consuming thirst of our great world-fever and just go along, with no secret heart's love reaching after any body, but whosoever longs to live in the bright cordiality of brotherhood, and have the true enjoyment of his kind, must atone himself into the gentleness and patience of love all the way.

<small>As with us, so with Christ.</small>

Doubtless it may seem to some to be a hard lot put upon us, which requires us to be not only well-doers, but atoners also—the world itself to be a kind of mutually atoning world—so that we have it put upon us, not only to suffer for our own sins, but also for the sins of those who do us injury. This, I say, will seem quite hard to many. But it will depend on what kind of world we require God to give us. If it must be a world made up of facilities, and favors, and all kinds of pleasantness, with no hurts suffered, no wrongs done, no liabilities of damage, no responsibilities of sacrifice, in a word, if there is to be no tragedy, or tragic side, in our life, but all sides smoothly rounded alike, then of course a plan that is to keep us all, and about all the time, at

<small>Our tragic element necessary.</small>

making cost in this manner for the forgiving of bad people, may take on a look very forbidding and tedious. And yet after all there is no imaginable world, I am quite sure, that has a thousandth part of the tedium in it which one would have that is wholly made up of delectations. Insipid, uneventful, flat, with no great sentiments in it, no heroic side in duty, nothing heroic any where, nothing to condemn that touches us, nothing to forgive because we are not touched—why, such a world would even die of inanity. No, let us have tragedy and a strong, large mixture of it. And then if we chance to be good—good enough to make loss for our enemies—what luxury shall we have in our forgivenesses and the great sentiments heaved up in us as in mighty exaltations, by our experience. Of course it is not to be charged against God that he makes the bad necessities of our very tragic life. The bad part of it is all from ourselves, and the grand atonings planned for, to be the universal element, are just that cost of experience in which we are most ennobled and blessed. Let me have the chance of forgiving my enemy, and I have more enlargement of life, a more uplifted consciousness, than if I owned the world in fee.

II.

Finding, in this manner, how our own moral nature, as such, becomes alienated and averted from them The great analogy stated. that do us wrong and trample the rights of others, and how it tones itself to a completely forgiving state only by acts of cost or sacrifice which are, in proper verity, propitiations of itself, it should not surprise us to find the analogy running far enough to comprehend all other moral natures, even the highest. And here, as I conceive, we get our initiatory point for the true understanding of the christian propitiation. We have only to go back on the pathologies of our own moral nature, to make the discovery that we ourselves instinctively make sacrifice, to gain our adversary; in doing which we also gain ourselves. I said that we do it instinctively, but I only mean that our moral instincts are so far cast in this mold as to induce this kind of action, when we are in the highest key of supernatural life and exaltation. I wish I could believe that we are always in this key; for it is the infelicity of my argument, in this great subject, that I am required to hang it on a fact, which alas! too many have no witness of in their own experience. And my fear is that the analogy I suggest will be quite insignificant to them, because they run their life on so low a key, and make it so nearly selfish, that the exalted consciousness, which is itself so near akin to God, is not on hand to second what I say. How shall it seem reasonable, or even properly intelligent, to propose the verification of God's way in forgiveness by our own, or the fact of his propitiation in order to his forgivenesses by the propitiation we instinctively make ready in our own, when the mind that is addressed lives in no element of forgiveness and propitiation, and has nothing in experience to make so high an ascription seem any thing better than a dull extravagance. Let the caution here given be taken without offense.

Still it will be something for such to observe how expressly and even formally the indorsement of revelation is given us, for just this free appeal to the human analogies. Thus when Christ bids us pray, "Forgive as we forgive," his apostle turns the doctrine boldly round, requiring us to forgive "even as God for Christ's sake hath forgiven us." By these words "for Christ's sake," *en Christō* or in Christ, he does not mean, as many understand, on the ground of satisfaction made by Christ—for we plainly enough can not make satisfaction for the sin of our enemy—but he means that we are to forgive, as volunteering in the cost of sacrifice, after Christ's example. Indeed there could be no forgiveness in God, on the ground of satisfaction; it would only be his admission that nothing is any longer due.

Let it not be suspected that we fall into a case of inversion here, that implies mistake in the argument; viz., that we conceive Christ in his forgivenesses, or his propitiation, to be following the type of ours. Causations and examples imply a state of priority or precedence, but a mere analogy does not. It only signifies that the two sides of it are in correspondence, no matter how. Christ, in all that pertains to his propitiation and his forgiveness to enemies, furnishes the ideas and helps we work by in ours, and we are even to allow that we have no complete adequacy without them; but our propitiations

No mistake in the analogy.

and forgivenesses, when these are wrought, suppose analogical properties in our very nature, by which Christ may set us on working correspondently with himself, and forgiving our enemies even as he does his.

Supposing now the fact of such constituent analogies existing both in us and him, certain questions will arise in pursuing the exposition proposed, that require to be answered.

1. Is it to be understood that Christ goes to the cross just to get the reaction of so great suffering on himself, and so to mitigate or propitiate his own feeling in the way of preparing to forgive? *Christ dies not for the reaction of it.* That would be a very constrained, self-attentive attitude, and we could not think of it with respect. No such thing is implied, or supposed in the human examples referred to. We do not ourselves go into sacrifice for our enemy to gain or soften ourselves, but only to help him in his trouble, and minister to his bad mind in ways that may gain him to repentance; every thing we do and suffer is for his benefit, or for effect on him, only it results that our sacrifice affects our mind or disposition also towards him. We are in a way of being completely reconciled to him, as we hope he sometime will be to us. The stress of all we do or suffer is for him, and in that consciousness it is that we are atoned, having all our aversions, disgusts, and condemnations liquefied, or dissolved away. In this there is nothing artificial or constrained; we are simply acting ourselves into forgiveness towards him in our endeavor

to bless him and bring him into a better mind towards us.

2. Is it objected that God loves his adversary already, and needs not love him more to forgive? Of course he needs not love him more, and it is no office of the propitiation to produce in him a greater love for that purpose. The propitiation itself proceeds from his love, and is only designed to work on other unreducible sentiments that hinder his love, in forgivenesses it might otherwise bestow. Our own love, as we saw, might be sufficient if it were not hindered by certain collateral, obstructive sentiments, and God is in this moral analogy with us. He is put in arms against wrong doers just as we are, by his moral disgusts, displeasures, abhorrences, indignations, revulsions, and what is more than all, by his offended holiness, and by force of these partly recalcitrant sentiments he is so far shut back, in the sympathies of his love, that he can nerve himself to the severities of government so long as such severities are wanted. He is not less perfect because these antagonistic sentiments are in him, but even more perfect than he would be without them; and a propitiation is required, not because they are bad, but only to move them aside when they are not wanted. They are never to be extirpated from the mind of God, but are always to be in him even as parts of his perfection; only they do not act uniformly into his character, but casually, when, all things considered, they should; just as we have casual factors letting in

God loves his adversary already.

their action here and there among the constant factors. God has it for a part of his liberty to be held by these casual factors when he should be, and not held when he can do better works for his repentant children by letting forgiveness take their place. Propitiation then, as the necessary precondition of forgiveness, supposes no necessity that God should be made better. And he will forgive without damage to his character, just when his love, in making cost for his enemy, gains that enemy to himself. The beauty of the true conception is that God is not obliged, by his side-factors or subordinate sentiments, to be everlastingly disgusted, revolted, heated with condemnation, but that he has self-government, and world government, and full liberty left him. His severities of sentiment remain, just as the Red Sea remained after the children of Israel passed through. And yet they had passed through.

3. It will be imagined, perhaps, by objectors of a different class, that God's holiness, or spiritual chastity, puts him in a condition where all the analogies of human forgiveness fail. *God's holiness does not put him out of analogy.* It is enough for us to be a little gentled in feeling, to make our forgivenesses flow. Whereas he must even morally wrong his own pure nature, to forgive any transgression without being satisfied for it—as he can be only when some other bears the offense and by adequate suffering atones it. That is, he can forgive sin only on receiving adequate pay! But we never propose that way of forgiveness

for our human enemy, restricted as we are in our holiness. It would even subject a man to ignominy to do it—all the more certainly if he is counted a specially holy man. It is very true that God's offense toward sin is deepest because of his holiness. But the depth of his holiness will match itself also in the depth of his forgiveness. And what do we see but that the holiest men, who are the men most deeply wounded by wrong, forgive most easily. God too holy to forgive an enemy! Rather judge that forgiveness is itself the supreme joy of holiness, whether in God or man.

4. It will be imagined that God is in a different case from us, in the fact that he maintains a government as we do not, and that he is therefore restricted in the matter of forgiveness by considerations of order and public authority, when we are not so restricted. Hence that we may be softened or propitiated towards our enemy by what we do to gain him, when God can not be without exacting somehow what the penal institute of the law requires. I shall have more to say of this when I come to speak in the next chapter of the necessities of Law. For the present I have these two points to put forward as being in themselves sufficient. First that no forgiveness, whether by man or God, obliterates the fact of a wrong, or at all salves the wounds of violated obligations. It operates only on, or between, the two parties personally. The bad act stands forever, plainly enough, for nothing can efface

God has government to maintain.

or any way alter what is done. The law and its sanctions also stand as immovable as the eternal morality. And the penal sanctions work on still in the man by natural causation after he is forgiven, till they are worn out or winnowed away by the supernatural causations of grace in his life. Add to this, secondly, that we as mortals do in fact govern with God, and are held to the maintenance of good government with him. Every law of his kingdom is ours. His governing interest is ours. We have the same reason to be jealous of wrong and shocked by disorder. We reign with him in fact in what is his Great Monarchy and our Republic, and we are just as free to forgive and be reconciled as He.

5. It may be objected that when we are propitiated towards our enemy, by the cost we make for him, the whole process takes place within ourselves, and the forgiving grace is not obtained of us by the intercession or mediation of another; whereas Christ obtains the forgiveness of sins for us by what he does before God, acting in our behalf. Even so, by acting before God; and yet not by acting before God and obtaining from God, as being strictly *other*. That would be tritheism and not trinity. Trinity makes him " same in substance," not other. We entirely misconceive this acting before God, when we make God one and Christ another acting in real otherhood before him. The three are still the one, and the three-folding is but a plural in so many finite forms, used representatively as person-

We only propitiate ourselves.

ations of the infinite One. Their very plurality implies their acting towards and before each other, in which they all become instrumentations for the one, but never, in any sense, other. If my right arm had grammatic personality in the same sense, it would be acting for me, or before me, but not doing any thing which I myself, the higher more inclusive substance, should not be doing for myself. We get vividness of conception for God by the representative action of the three; and God as infinite substance could not otherwise be set forth. They are above and below, supreme and subject, sending and sent, moving in space, taking human body and laying it off, acting before, and for, and with, in nature and into nature, but when these grammatic personalities are all resolved in their representative import, God is one, only so much better known. Hence, or in this view, Dr. Shedd was right, if only his theory had been right in other respects, when he conceived God as laying his wrath upon himself, punishing himself, satisfying his own justice out of his own pangs—"himself the judge, himself the priest, himself the sacrifice." And the old reformer, John Wessel, is even more explicit in his confession, saying—"God himself, himself the priest, himself the victim, for himself, of himself, to himself, made the satisfaction."* It is no fault therefore in this behalf that the analogy we draw from ourselves, only shows us working out a propitiation in ourselves. Christ is not other than

---

* *De causis incarnationis;* c. 17.

God in any such way that his propitiation is any the less truly a self-propitiation of God.

6. But it may be urged with emphasis and high confidence by some, as being a great derogation from God's honor, to suppose that he is held in detention, as respects forgiveness, till he has first mitigated his opposing sentiments, or let Christ do it by suffering and sacrifice in his behalf. That there is nothing to support this objection was just now sufficiently shown; for that which obstructs forgiveness in him is not something wherein he is less good than he should be, or something wherein he requires to be made better. The propitiation only takes away out of range certain subordinate and partly casual sentiments that wait on God's absolute principles and purposes, to act as displeasures and revulsions may in the toning of his legal discipline, and act no longer when their dominating force may properly cease.

No derogation from God's honor.

However, I perceive that speculation will easily twist this answer out of its proprieties, by questioning as to that little word *when*—Is it true that God must be gained or tempered transactionally, that is by acts in time, in order to the letting forth of grace upon his enemies? Certainly not; there is no such thing as date in God's dispositions. They are not dead fact, but living factors in his living nature. They condition each other, as the brain conditions breathing, and breathing the brain, being such as he generates everlastingly between what he feels and what he wills. Without such consideration, we seem to be imagining often that Christ has come into the world to make God better, and we very nearly say or sing it in a supposed key of orthodoxy; but if we understand him rather as having come to show us how God is acting himself always into the great time-currents of our story, we shall think him far more worthily. For his dispositions towards sin are shaped and colored everlastingly by what he thinks of it, and inwardly contrives and does and suffers for it. And his blessed forgivenesses were all in him, and ready grown, before Christ arrived, and before the world was made; and what he does among us by his sacrifice is to have its value in revealing, under time, how by sacrifice and much cost above time, the divine charities were always mitigating his dispositions and flowing out, as it were, by anticipation subduingly on his enemies. The transactional matter of Christ's life and death is a specimen chapter, so to speak, of the infinite book that records the eternal going on of God's blessed nature within. Being made in his image, we are able to see his moral dispositions, always forging their forgivenesses, under the reactions of endurance and sacrifice, as we do ours. And this is the eternal story of which Christ shows us but a single leaf.

<small>God's propitiations above time.</small>

Beheld in its outward human incidents, it is the tragedy of the love of God. And the dispositions of God are so wrought up in it, that he is seen embracing, not the lovely only, as we are wont to speak, when we imagine or teach that love is begotten by loveliness, but embracing the bad or unlovely in proffers beforehand of forgiveness. Most human love is unsacrificial love, thinking only to make fit answer to the lovable. We never go beyond this, till we make loss, and sacrifice, and cost, for some adversary of ours, or of goodness. By these propitiated, we forgive. All God's forgiving dispositions are dateless, and are cast in this mold. The Lambhood nature is in him, and the cross set up, before the incarnate Son arrives. His own love bows itself to endurance, by the prescriptive habit of his eternity, and the forgivenesses shown us in their formative era, so to speak, under the great transaction of Calvary, are in fact the everlasting predispositions of his nature. The cross, *ab æterno*, is in them—" the Lamb that was slain from the foundation of the world."

We can not have a God in fit sensibility unless the ante-mundane touch of it is in him. He can not be a forgiving God, if he is yet to begin the making cost for an enemy. A God therefore whose eternity has been impassible, untouched by suffering experience, will never be at all relational to my experience. He is wood, he is granite, or no better. What can he do for me, when he can not feel me? and what can I offer him, when he can not feel what I offer? If he is pleased with my good, he must have some feeling of my not good, and that is dis-pleasure, which is so far suffering. Just consider at this gate, as it opens, what a living God must suffer and be suffering always in his good sensibility. He pities, and pity going through a bad soul or body, by inward inspection, has how much to look upon that is painful. He abhors a wicked and cruel soul, and what is abhorrence but a recoil that is, at least etymologically, related to horror. In a vile and filthy mind he encounters disgust, and what is that but to suffer? All the persecutions of his friends, all the rage and scoffing of his enemies, all the hate and hatefulness of natures made for love, all desecrations of his honor, all perversions of his truth, impurity, lust, diseased inheritance—what are all these things to God's pure sensibility, since he has it, but evils to bear, offenses to suffer, such as can be forgiven only by a nature whose dispositions have been configured to sacrifice and cost, before the worlds were made. It is in God's character everlastingly, if we should not rather say his nature, to be always enduring the bad in their badness, and so melting his way lovingly through into forgiveness. Benefactor thus to all, and king of joy as of sorrow to himself. If his streams ran all one way, he would be too simply placid to be great, but he lives in everlasting countertides of struggle and victory—victory both over enemies without and violated good in himself. What is to come of all moral natures created, he well understood before their creation, and he peopled the world with them as one girding himself for war; that is, to live and reign by the mastery of their evil, including all the disasters to feeling in which evil comes. Thus he began early, as it were, in affliction for the bad, or only partly good; for " in their affliction he was afflicted, and he bare and carried them all the days of old." And so along down through the smoke of the ages—why not say of the eternities—he has been joyously "enduring the contradiction of sinners against himself," propitiated by his endurances, and so at all times ready to forgive their sin. And this exactly is the truth that Christ impresses by the affectingly beautiful short chapter of his story—it is the inward going on of God's nature in the sacrifices of love. He hates and abhors as we do, only never with a trace of malignity. His indignations burn hot against the outrages of wrong; just as in what we call our remorse, it is the terrible *orgē* of our own bosom that scorches and scathes our sin, doing it, as it were, benignantly and without injustice. So in respect of all God's sensibilities, forgivenesses, and sacrifices.*

III.

Having made our statement thus of the christian forgiveness and propitiation, interpreted and represented by analogies in our own human sentiment and practice, it now remains, going into the scripture, to find how far we are borne out by it in the doctrine proposed. Everything turns here, it will be discovered, on the meaning of sacrifice. And we have three sets of words, in our three scripture languages, the Hebrew, the Greek, and the English, in and by which the meaning is to be determined. In the Hebrew scriptures the word is

The scripture statement.

---
* Note 2.

uniformly *kaphar*. This is translated in the Septuagint and the New Testament by *hilaskomai*. And this again is translated in the English by *reconciliation, atonement,* and *propitiation;* by the first in a very few cases only; by the second almost uniformly in the English Old Testament; by the third as uniformly in the English New Testament. Only the New Testament has the word reconciliation, several times over; translating, however, another and wholly different word, that has no altar significance at all, and is therefore to be wholly disregarded in the inquest we are making.

We begin then at the Hebrew word *kaphar*, which is, in fact, the English word *cover*, the idea being that the sin is covered, hid, taken away by the sacrifice. And this idea it will be seen is not far off from the idea of a smoothing away of the offense, a mitigation, a placation, a propitiation of the mind offended, which appears to be an element of meaning always present in the uses of the word. Thus if we step aside in the Old Testament from the altar uses of this word, we fall on examples, in common life, where

Usus loquendi decisive. the real *usus loquendi* is plainly discovered; as when Jacob says, sending on his drove to meet Esau, his righteously offended brother; " I will *appease* him with the present that goeth before me."[*] The word of appeasement or propitiation here is *kaphar*, the altar word, showing beyond a question, what ideas or impressions it has

---

[*] Gen. xxxii, 20.

there carried. We have another example of the same word exactly correspondent: "The wrath of a king is as messengers of death, but a wise man will *pacify* it."* Here the smoothing, mitigating, mollifying, placating element is conspicuous as before.

Passing next to the Greek word of the New Testament, by which the Hebrew *kaphar* is translated, we look again for the true *usus loquendi*, to examples not occurring at the altar and under the altar forms, because collateral examples are a great deal more significant and decisive as to the true genius of the word. Thus we fall on the prayer of the publican—†" God be *merciful* to me a sinner." Here the " be merciful " is the old altar word of sacrifice *hilaskomai* used in the Passive Imperative, saying literally, " be thou propitiated, or propitiate thyself, bend thyself on me in forgiveness "—showing very clearly how the element of placation, or propitiation, has been connected always with the word in the uses of the altar. We also discover a little way off two cousins in the family of *hilaskomai*, *hileōs* and *anileōs* which may be taken as witnesses to the dispositions of the family. Thus we read, ‡" I will be *merciful* [propitiated in feeling] to their unrighteousness." And again §" he shall have judgment without mercy " [unmitigated, *unappeased* judgment] " that showed no mercy."

As regards the English words that are used to represent the two Hebrew and Greek words, the re

---
* Prov. xvi, 14. † Luke xviii, 13. ‡ Heb. viii, 12. § James ii, 13.

markable thing is that they so nearly agree. Thus the word reconciliation employed in translation, to carry a meaning that belongs to the altar, has the element of conciliation visible on its face. As when we read, "to make an end of sins, and to make reconciliation for iniquity, and to bring in everlasting righteousness," the meaning would not be essentially different if it were written "to make propitiation for iniquity."* The word *atonement*, more frequently used, carries the same element of conciliation or propitiation in a different manner by just naming the results; that is to *at-one;* for this is the old English word in the old English way of printing, and the word, in that original use, never meant, as now, *to make amends*, which is a perfectly unchristian use, but to gather into accord as by love and cost and heavy expense of feeling. The New Testament English word *propitiation* coincides with these other two, without more than a shade of difference.

We are ready therefore now, after sifting all these words with as much of accuracy as we are able, to go back first upon the Old Testament sacrifice and settle the significance of it, showing also how, or by what means, it obtained that significance. And here the first thing to be noted is that it makes nothing of the pain of the victim. Nothing is ever done to increase the pain of the animal when slain, and there is never any thing

<small>Old Testament sacrifices.</small>

---

* Daniel ix, 24.

said which indicates the least mental attention to it. The pain is plainly a matter of supreme indifference. The next thing is, that there is no vestige of retributive quality in the sacrifice. The smoke is to be rolled up as a sweet smelling savor, and not as a smoke of retribution. The associations never once suggest retribution. Thirdly, there is no compensation in the sacrifices. They are never proposed in a way of payment, or of obligation compounded. They are not satisfactions, nor any way linked with ideas of satisfaction—no man's lamb pays for his sin. Fourthly, they are never offered as a legal substitution. There is a certain mystic and ritual way of substitution practiced indeed, as when the worshiper puts his hands on the head of the sacrifice, or on the head of the goat, driven out to signify the deportation of his sin, but nobody ever imagines, unless it be to make out some point of theology, that the animal is held in legal substitution. To have the sins legally on him, the goat must be a legal subject, else they are as little on him as they would be on a barrow or a cart. Doubtless they are on him in a figure, and then of course their deportation is signified in a figure—the reality of which will be, that the faith of the transgressor makes what he is thereby helped to believe, an actual and free deliverance.

But what of the blood? for the sacrifice is a rite of blood; as if it were not in God's nature, some shallow casuist will often object, to be any more pacified towards sin, or at all mitigated in his wrath, except by the sight of blood! Somebody, that is, must bleed for it, else there is no forgiveness. In which way of speaking, the impression is that blood comes into the sacrifice invested with all our freezing conceptions of guilt, because no otherwise but by its horror-dripping stains could God find fit expression made in the sacrifice, of our detestation of the sin we come to have forgiven. But we greatly mistake if we suppose that any so delicate impression of blood was ever felt among those old pasture-men of the East, with whom sacrifice began; accustomed as they were to the killing of some animal from their herds, at their tent door, three or four times a day, and trained to use the knife even from childhood. But there was a more genuine, really delicate impression of blood prepared in their minds, by artificial, institutional causes, which having been prepared for that purpose, *were* the reason why so much is made of bleeding and blood in the sacrifices. The problem was to make the sacrifice a power, by collecting about the victim intensely sacred impressions. And to this end a statute was passed concerning blood, at a very early period, which was in fact the fountain of all meaning in sacrifice, even down to the sacrifice of Christ himself.* "For the life of the flesh is in the blood, and I have given it to you upon the altar to make an

No demand of blood as blood.

Blood made sacred for the altar.

---

* Lev. xvii, 11, 12, and 14.

atonement [or propitiation] for your souls; for it is the blood that maketh an atonement for the soul. Therefore I said unto the children of Israel, No soul of you shall eat blood. Whosoever eateth it shall be cut off." These worshipers of the old time took nothing in their religious experience by definition or analysis, they experienced only what they saw or acted. And God gave them a symbol of something sacred by which to come before him, viz., blood made sacred by being separated from every other use; the idea being that, in having offered their holiest and best thing to God, they have made an expression that carries the strongest sense of their sin, and will most certainly conciliate the offended purity of God. They have offered up even life, that mystic power enshrined in blood, the deepest, holiest secret of the creation, more significant than all the most hidden treasures and choicest gems of the world. Bähr, who has carefully investigated the ancient statute just cited, makes the sacrifice "an appointment of God, to signify the yielding up of the soul of the sacrificer (symbolized by the blood or life of the victim) to God as a condition of acceptance." But it needs to be added after this, that there is a power and value in the blood of the rite, over and above what it signifies to the worshiper in the matter of his own particular use as moving from himself. For God ordains the offering, and it is God that puts the life in the blood, and hedges about the blood with all most scrupulous sanctities, for the fit impression of the worshiper, and also for his own high part in it. And he it is that says—I have given it to you upon the altar; for it is to be the token also of *my* cost, and of what I have been pledged, from all past ages downward, to accomplish for the forgiveness of the sins of the world. In this giving up of blood and life behold what I will sometime do for the reconciling of transgression. Let this seem to be only a conceit, if any one please, for it is not said in words, but time will by and by say it loud enough to end all doubt. For whether we imagine it or not, this rite of sacrifice begun, this bleeding-out of sacred life, is going shortly to be lifted in its range, and it has been ordered in the main for that very purpose. Just as all the higher, finer words of our dictionaries climb up out of low base levels in things, and take significances rich enough for their ennobled service. What if there chance to be something here, in this humble offering of lambs, that will sometime be made to represent the sacred and dear life of Christ, offered up at greater cost to God's feeling than any thing ever was or could be to ours. And what if that simple designation "Lamb of God that taketh away the sin of the world"—defining nothing, spinning no analogies—were just wept into the world's heart and left to quicken the feeling of a new life, how certainly would the sinning myriads of the world begin to confess, This surely is the body that was prepared, this must be the atonement indeed.

Even so! this is the Sacrifice that all sacrifices were

looking after and climbing up to behold. They were
the literal base-level sacrifices, offered
by priests and by fire upon an altar, *Figures of the true sacrifice.*
atoning the man by what he offered, and also God by
implication—engaged to be atoned on his part by
these hallowed symbols of cost, in the blood and the
life. Whereas in that other better Lamb of Sacrifice,
that really true sacrifice that was foreshadowed, there
is neither any lamb at all nor any sacrifice, and it is
only meant to be a sacrifice a great way out of correspondence, that we may not class it, too closely,
with the very dull and prosy rites which have had
their uses now fulfilled, in preparing a language for
something more significant and in a higher key. The
real truth, if we tell it as it is, makes the sacrifice a
murder, and the blood on Calvary the blood of murder: there is no altar, no fire, no priest; it is simply
the act of a mob outside of the temple and the city,
gibbeting the Sacred Life yielded up to their fury.
And what they have done is called the sacrifice, in a
word that would even be irony, if it did not cover
the awfully transcendent, interior fact, of a cost so
terrible, endured by the feeling of God. This is the
blood, and this the life, expected of old, when the
blood and the life were consecrated by the statute of
the altar. Looking on here with our eyes, we see
nothing religious, even the offering is wholly blank
to us, only that the world itself, shuddering and dark-
ening into night, tries visibly to be telling us something of it, if it could! There is at any rate no

atonement in the form. The blood of the murder buys nothing as in pay, wins nothing as by suit or compensation, mitigates no feeling of God that we can see, as by intercession before him; and yet there is to God, in his own deep nature, a propitiation accomplished for sin, because of the divine Lambhood that has been lovingly offered in the smoke of so fierce transgression.

Our scripture excursion comes round finally, after the wide range taken, to be concluded by the famous full-period text of Paul in his epistle to the Romans, "Whom God hath set forth to be a propitiation, through faith in his blood,"* &c. I do not cite the whole passage, but only the first two clauses, reserving the part that is left to be used hereafter, when the matter of justification is to be discussed. Three points noted, in the briefest manner possible, will sufficiently indicate the import of the words. (1.) There is a propitiation accomplished in Christ's life, and especially in his very tragic death, which prepares a way of forgiveness for the sins of the world. The forgiveness now will be more than verbal, it will be real, clean, complete. (2.) It is God himself who is forward in this transaction— "Whom God hath set forth." It is not Pilate who has done it, not Caiaphas, nor the soldiers, but it is that God has suffered them so far to make irruption upon his throne, and pluck down him, who by the determinate counsel and foreknowledge was delivered

So comes the propitiation.

---

* Romans iii, 25.

into their hands; for how can it be imagined what the propitiation can do, save as it is set forth by the worst that sin can do, worsted itself in turn by the blood of its crime? And (3) this propitiation is to be received only by faith—a " propitiation through faith in his blood." For it is this faith in fact which makes the murder a sacrifice; which it does by accepting it as the sacred altar-blood and life, and beholding in it that sublime act of cost, in which God has bent himself downward, in loss and sorrow, over the hard face of sin, to say, and saying to make good, " thy sins are forgiven thee."

IV.

The propitiation that was necessary to forgiveness we have now discovered and constructively verified, under its human analogies; but there is a very important objection to propitiation itself that requires to be removed—an objection that is incurred by every scheme which assumes the word propitiation, as truly as by that which I have here proposed. *A great standing objection.* The need of any such mitigation or amendment in God's dispositions, supposes, it is often maintained, to just the same extent, his spiritual defectiveness; and the fact of his being thus amended by a transaction in time, supposes an improvement, to the same degree, and a correspondent derogation from the stability or immutability of his character. I have been discussing, before, an objection closely related to this, and yet very different.

There the question was how God can have his dignity, when he is supposed to be transactionally mitigated by what is done or suffered in time? Here the question is, how he can have his dignity, when his eternal mind itself requires to be propitiated, in order to the supreme act of goodness to an enemy. The argument of the two questions, wide apart as they are in their nature, runs more nearly in the same vein than might be wished. But the objections themselves are so very important, that small varieties of treatment may have their use. I have said already that the propitiation, so called, is not a fact accomplished in time, but an historic matter represented in that way, to exhibit the interior, ante-mundane, eternally-proceeding sacrifice of the Lamb that was slain before the foundation of the world. In saying this I am not striking the predestination string of Calvinism, but am simply finding how the everlasting God, in a particular year of the calendar, viz., the year of Christ's death, was gained *representatively* to new dispositions, and became, in some new sense, a Saviour—incredible, impossible as it may seem—and how, in fact, he proved himself the more grandly, in that he here sets forth in time and story, what occupies, and fills, and glorifies, the whole interior working of his own eternity, and could by no other method be fitly revealed to mortal apprehension. The great salvation was not, in this view, wrought by the new composure of God in that particular year, but it was set forth as an everlasting new composure, so to speak, made evident in that year's doings—"Whom God hath set forth to be a propitiation, through faith in his blood, to declare his righteousness in the remission of sins that are past, through the forbearance of God." Faith only sees, in the outward blessing of to-day, what covers matter going on before, in the eternal, inward proceeding of his mind towards human creatures and affairs.

Now if it shall seem to some that, in thus removing our objection, we very nearly make a nullity of the gospel itself, reducing it to a fact significant in what it shows only, and not in what it is or does, I will not stop to inquire how far the same kind of doubt hangs over every thing, but will hasten to concede that a great part of mankind, trained to no such modes of thought, will undoubtedly best appropriate the gospel, by keeping down as closely as possible on the level of a transaction in time. Indeed, there is some doubt how far it may be needed for us all, to stay by the historic forms, and see the gospel done transactionally in time—to hear the word of Jesus, watch his healings, read his face, study his masterhood, bow down with him in Gethsemane, die with him on the cross—only we may have it as our privilege, I think, when our mind recoils from the tremendous difficulty of propitiation itself, to carry the whole matter up above the ranges of time, and look on him who stands there "in the midst of the throne, as it had been a Lamb slain from the foundation of the world."

But there is yet another way, if really it be another,

<small>Another solution.</small> as I think it is, of removing this, to some it may be, rather intractable objection. We do not properly conceive God's attributes, when we pack them as so many solid blocks of perfection in his perfect nature. Least of all do we fitly conceive his sentiments and dispositions in that manner. If we take his wrath-principle as one block, calling it his justice; his omnipotence as another, able to do any thing which can be thought; his will-principle as another, essentially autocratic and absolute; his hatred-of-wrong-principle, in deifically fixed animosity, as another; and then if we bring in the patiences, and tender charities, and the vicariously suffering grace, it will be very difficult to make blocks of them any way, and, when they flow in through the interstices, they will have power to move, configure, combine, compelling all the others to offer them a yielding side, and to come into a newly constructed whole. Indeed, it will begin to be as if they were all being propitiated. They are no more blocks, in fact, but elements of life rather, flowing pervasively into, and among, and over, and under, and through, one another—liquids all, flowing in to liquefy, and temper, and color, and sweeten each other, in such way as to compose a perfect rule, and a grand harmonic character. And this harmonic character will so be cast as to keep all purpose, sentiment, and disposition chiming with the wants, conditions, wrongs, relentings, personal affections, providential

changes, and prayers of the world. And what have we thus, in the eternal going on of God's interior nature, but an eternal going on of propitiations, ready for every human creature in his time.

It may occur to some as a very strange thing, amounting, in fact, to another objection, that God should be any way restricted in his forgivenesses, when the mere instinct of kind or natural paternity is so free, and drops out all displeasures with such prompt facility. Why is *God has no reluctance here.* God to be gained as one who forgives reluctantly? Should not such a being have his pardons ready beforehand? Why, a human mother in her simple, motherhood nature—is she not good enough to forgive an erring son, without parley, or without a question? She may do it, I answer, simply because she is not good enough to raise the parley, or to make it a moral affair at all, when of course it is not forgiveness. In every true moral transaction the thing done is made ready by moral dispositions prepared for it. Let us not be in haste to measure God's forgivenesses by the mother-pardon spilled on a reprobate son. Expecting in God what we boast in her, we should certainly do Him great irreverence. As if the mere maternity of natural instinct, having no moral ingredient whatever, could be cited as a match and parallel for the clean, everlastingly sealed acceptance, and moral embrace of God. Just contrary to this, the wrath or offended holiness, the pure sensibilities, shocked by disgust, the moral repugnances and dis-

7*

pleasures, the immovable indignations, must not hurry to clasp a wild and filthy reprobate. Probably God has nature-sentiment enough in him to do even that, but so far and in that point of view, he would really need to be made better; to go up out of his nature-plane into the moral, and prepare a moral settlement based in a moral forgiveness. And yet as we have said many times over, he has done it—did it eternal ages ago—moving so promptly and with such spontaneous facility that the grace is ready long before the man arrives to receive it. If there is any look of reluctance in the matter, it is that the propitiation requires to be revealed by a transactional process, and that the subjects to be forgiven are so very slow in coming to the point of faith that makes forgiveness possible. And yet, though done as in the general and before time, it is a grace so personally guaged and tempered when it is inwardly pronounced, that each may say, along down the ages, with even a better right than if the Master had kissed a farewell on his cheek—"who loved me and gave himself for me."

Closing here my argument for the propitiation, I think I shall be permitted to speak of the religious benefits to be expected from the worthier and better ideal conceptions of God, that will of course go with it and keep it company. Every strongly variant or peculiar type of thought concerning God, carries with it an ideal of God proper only to itself. Thus from his creatorship, and especially from the great and scientific, world-

Ideals of God.

massing facts of astronomy, we are set upon the idealizing of God as a being omnipotent. And so strong is the impression we receive, that it not unlikely gulfs every other, even the impression of his responsibility to right. He becomes, in chief significance, the Almighty, and what after that, many are not much concerned to know. All theological questions involved in human liberty, are brought to an end, by the fact that God can do any thing which either he or we can think. In the same way, it is often declared to be the praise of Calvinism that it makes God "big" by the autocratic rule of his decrees and predestinations. So that holding us fast in the vise of his sovereignty, and bending us down always under the overhang of his will, the awful discipline makes imprints of authority and law, that fasten immovably both society and religion. Again there is a certain ideal of God which is raised by our orthodox modes of legal atonement, such as deal in substituted punishment, satisfactions of justice, compensations, governmental equivalents, remissions bought and paid for—where nothing turns upon a sympathy or feeling, but every thing on a computative calculation, sharpened to the point of a jot or tittle of the law. Here the ideal raised is that of an exact or stringently exacting God, and the impression is not altogether ill, if it were not so far mixed with offense as to cause revulsion only, in all the broadly generous, thoughtfully circumspect natures. Another ideal of God, much valued by many, does not come in as a resultant, but is directly chosen for its own sake, and is called the Fatherhood of God. It has the merit of raising no offense, but there is such a certainty of diminution for God in any merely human type of paternity, that he is too inefficiently conceived in it for any strain of high-going rule or endeavor. What I am here proposing in the way of propitiation begins at the summit of God's eternity, where he lets in sorrow in the right of his supremacy, bathing his will in it when he reigns, recognizing always, and expecting always to recognize, the fact that it belongs to every moral nature, as truly to atone its adversaries, as to observe equity with its friends. He is brought down thus, or, shall we rather say? brought up, before the worlds are made, into the Passive Virtues. For he it is that accepts them by spontaneous choice, in advance of all creatures, and counts all other good too dry for joy without them. They are with him in the beginning of his way, and before his works of old. He creates the world thus in their counsel, consenting to have it on hand as a bad world, because in them he has found a ransom. The dread possibility of sin, incidental to the existence of moral natures, does not prevent his act of creation; for his great love wants them nigh, and the Patience of Sins is in him, able to bear the cost of their undoing and deliverance; so that when the outbreak comes, he is able to let it be, able to suffer it and for it, able to rule it, in the Kingly Majesty of his Patience.

V.

To avoid the confusion that might be created by bringing into my argument another and very different matter, and having on hand for discussion two important issues at once, I have carried along the great subject of propitiation to its final conclusion by itself. Still my argument is not finished when I thus ignore the other issue referred to, and pass it wholly by without notice or attention. I go back, therefore, now to the point where that other question might have come forward also to claim its part in the discussion, and resume the investigation at that point. Having found that the two words of sacrifice in the Hebrew and Greek scriptures, *kaphar* and *hilaskomai*, bear a sense of mitigation, and in that manner of propitiation, I considered the latter to be sufficiently established as the meaning also of the christian sacrifice. But it happens that the Greek word is used also in the classics, where I am not able to deny that it is largely or quite commonly used to signify expiation. And so the question is raised whether, after all, expiation is not a meaning in these words, compatible with the Scripture uses. In this manner we have the question, Propitiation, or Expiation? back upon us in the alternative, and the whole budget of doubt is loose again.

What of expiation.

We are also the more heavily pressed by the question in this form, that our orthodox theologians and confessions are all the while saying *expiation* for the christian sacrifice, without any apparent suspicion of impropriety. They even go to the classic historians and poets, to cite instances of expiation as proofs of the necessity of sacrifice, and do it without any misgiving or scruple. Happily our English scriptures are clear of this impeachment, for the word *expiation* is not once found in them.* Indeed, I think our English translators are shy of so heathenish a word, as they very well might be.

<small>We go to the classics.</small>

In the facts that are classed as expiations, there is of course a very great diversity, but they are discovered, when closely examined, to be all alike defective in principle. We may take as a worst and most shocking example, the spectacle of human fathers and mothers whipping their children through beds of fire, to please some god who is turning plague, or battle, or weather against them. Or if we prefer to look on a best example rather, I remember no instance at all comparable, in dignity or benignity, with the legend of the Roman Curtius, plunging headlong man and horse into the gulf which had opened in the ground of the forum, and which it was declared, by some oracle, should never be closed till the glory of Rome was thrown into it. A truly grand patriot we have in the

<small>Worst and best examples.</small>

---

* It is supposed to have come into English from the Vulgate, and not till shortly after the translation. However, the translators, who learned half their theology from the Latin, must have been familiar with it.

man; who would yet have been as much more ennobled if he could have seen how mean the oracle, and contemptible the god, and stood back from the sacrifice. Clearly enough there is nothing to be carried back into christianity from such examples. A suffusion of the mere idea breeds inevitable confusion in the doctrine, and a great part of the trouble we have in our efforts to settle the christian truth, is caused by the admission of this false element.

The divergence it creates begins to be evident, when it is observed that we propitiate only a person, and expiate only a fact, or act, or thing; winning, it may be, any sort of favor, good or bad, by the pains undergone. Propitiation seeks the preparing always of a disposition morally right and good. Expiation is indifferent, caring never for the morality or justice of what is gained, but only for the agreeableness of it. *What expiation does.* No righteous being or god is propitiated by any contribution of pains, as being pains, or by any kind of naked suffering; but such pains are good in expiation according to the temper of the god, no matter what the motive, or the meaning, in which they are offered. The christian sacrifice of propitiation, we are told, is offered, or set forth, "to declare the righteousness of God," and to gain all such as will believe in it to a new life quickened in righteousness. In the expiations of the heathen peoples the main thing is to have enough suffered, for the apprehended wrath will be stayed when the rages of the gods are glutted. No new relationship in character is expected, no ingenerated righteousness in the life, the distinctive idea being that the god offended is to have an evil given him by consent, for an evil due by retribution, or feared from his tokens of exasperation. It throws in before God, or the gods, some deprecating evil, in the expectation that the wrath may be satisfied by its compensation. The power of the expiation depends not on the sentiments, or repentances, or pious intentions connected with it, but entirely on the voluntary damage incurred in it. According to the Latin idea, *Diis violatis expiatio debetur*—"when the gods are wronged, expiation is their due"—and the understanding is that, when the wrong-doers punish themselves in great losses, it buys off the wrath of the gods and turns them to the side of favor.

The pagan religions were corruptions, plainly enough in this view, of the original, ante-Mosaic, *cultus*—superstitions of degenerate brood, such as guilt, and fear, and the spurious motherhood of ignorance, have it for their law to propagate. As repentance settles into penance under this regimen of superstition, so the sacrifices settled into expiations under the same. And the process only went a little farther, when they fell, as they did the pagan world over, into the practice of human sacrifices; for since the gods were to be gained by expiatory evils, the greater the evil the more sure the favor; and therefore they sometimes offered their captives, sometimes their sons and daughters, counting it possible in no other manner, to sufficiently placate their envious and bloody deities. Expiation figured in this manner, not as a merely casual and occasional part of religion, but as being very nearly the same thing as religion itself. For as Tacitus could say, that "the gods interfere in human concerns but to punish," what could men think of doing, in religion, but to expiate?

How low the pitch given to religion must be, under such rites, maintained for such purposes, may be seen from the fact that *Expiation demoralizes.* almost never, in the expiations offered as in deprecation of hostility and wrath on the part of the gods appealed to, is any least consideration had of their character. They are even thought to be unsaintly and base, actuated by jealousy of other gods, working in revenge, and lust, and deceit. As to their justice, nobody thinks of it, and the question never is, how to make good before them any fault of crime or personal misconduct. The expiation has commonly no fairer chance because it makes suit to the virtue of the god; on the contrary, any most politic scheme to get the advance of an adversary, in coming at the cunning deity's favor, promises not only as well as a more timidly conscientious appeal, but even better. Every one, at all versed in the classics, perfectly well knows that getting beforehand with the gods is the main thing in expiations. Their very smoke is the smoke of stratagem. The devotees and the gods are for the most part liars and cheats together. Nobody has any doubt of it, or conscience concerning it, and the integrity of the heathen world in general is just so far labefact, prostitute, and morally rotted away, as it has religiously abounded in expiations. And yet how many christian teachers and disciples imagine that our gospel is to have its gain by following the classic expiations, and that the law and justice of God are to be rightly seconded by their example! Are not classic authorities good? And is not our religion finely complimented by them?

At the same time it is not to be denied that, drawing back from the field of the classics into the field of Scripture, it is possible there to hold a severer and more nearly moral view of sacrifices, which still classes them as expiations.

Expiation as accepted evil.

Sin being a violation of the law of God, incurs, in that manner, a dread liability of pain or punishment, and sacrifices, it is conceived, make satisfaction to God for the offense and consequent bad liability, obtaining, in that manner, a just release. Thus a third party, Christ himself, comes in to offer the suffering of pain as an evil, which is accepted as being a good enough match for the evil that is due. In this manner, he makes amends for the sin by evil paid for evil due, and that is expiation. But the scheme, if not immoral, is fairly unmoral, as it ought to be under that word; showing that God accepts the pains of the good in payment for the pains of the bad, and is more intent on getting his modicum of pains than he is on having proper justice done—taking clean away the word and fact of forgiveness; for if the debt of sin is paid, there is no longer any thing to forgive; substituting government also by a kind of proceeding that has no relation whatever to conscience and right. Happily there is not a single case of expiation in the whole christian scriptures, or any thing in the scripture sacrifices which bears a look that way, significant enough to support an argument. To verify this fact, I would go over a complete revision, if I had the time, as I did in my former treatise; but I think it will suffice just to recapitulate the points which any one may establish by a very brief examination.

Nothing is ever made in the sacrifices, as I have already observed, of the pains of the animal. The occasion itself is very generally regarded as a festive occasion, and the sacrifices are called "sacrifices of joy." And it is a very singular fact to be historically accounted for, that two of our most merrily jocund words in English are lineal descendants of the same stock with the altar word *hilaskomai*, and related of course in meaning. I speak of the words *hilarity* and *exhilaration;* which if they somewhat overdo the gladness and emancipative grace of propitiation, very plainly never felt the touch of pains and penalties, so greatly magnified in expiation. Abraham was put through a trial of sacrifice; or rather was not put through, but stopped short in the midst of it, to learn that a sheep is better than a man for the offering; with a deliberate view, no doubt, to his being set up in his family, for

<small>No instances in the Scripture.</small>

all future time, as a bulwark against the unnatural and monstrous practice of human sacrifice, which was getting to be the distinctive practice of his time. There is no trace of expiation in the passover-rite; which, considering that it is the original of the Lord's Supper, makes it the more remarkable; since plainly there is some reference in the supper to pains endured, though endured, as the apostle teaches, not for pay but for propitiation.

Expiations never occur on occasions where we most naturally look for them; as in the judgment of Korah where there is an outbreak of mutiny and riotous tumult, and where, as we half naturally judge, a considerable smart of expiation might cool the rage of their fever. By and by, in the progress of the story, it begins to look as if the sacrifices were outgrown, and the human sacrifices of the heathen are sharply rebuked; "To what purpose is the multitude of your sacrifices? Bring no more vain oblations. Wash you, make you clean." So speaks the great preacher Isaiah, and Micah follows in a strain equally pungent—"Will the Lord be pleased with thousands of rams, or with tens of thousands of rivers of oil? Shall I give my first born for my transgression, the fruit of my body for the sin of my soul? What doth the Lord require of thee, O man, but to do justly, and to love mercy, and to walk humbly with thy God?" Once more, we discover that a certain day is appointed to be observed, every year, by the people, which is to be the specially serious day of their calendar. It is to be a day of abstinence and deep thoughtfulness, in which the whole nation, considered as being unclean in every faculty and sense—in their houses, their worship, their priesthood, and their very altars—is to undergo a complete lustration and come forth clean. "On that day shall the priest make atonement for you, to cleanse you, that ye may be clean from all your sins before the Lord."* The atonement, it will be observed, is lustral and not expiatory—"an atonement for you to cleanse you." This religious day is generally called, especially by the Jews, their great day of expiation, though never as holding the term in any closely defined meaning. The day is deeply serious and very impressive, but there is really nothing in it that has any least appearance of penality, or of evil suffered to make amends for evil done.

In this sketch I think it will sufficiently appear that expiatory suffering is not a scripture idea. To further extend the argument is unnecessary. It was clear enough in the beginning, that one or the other, propitiation or expiation, must go down; the two being morally incompatible. Which of the two it must be, I think we now have no room left for doubt. If the moral pitch of our gospel is low enough to be satisfied with a bought salvation, quantitatively suffered for, and paid up as in expiation, it certainly can not rise high enough to even think a salvation unbought, yet distilled in that great alembic of cost-making love wherein God prepares the recon-

---

* Com. Lev. xvi.

ciliation of his enemies. If, on the contrary, it is in a pitch of character high enough to conceive the transcendent movements of propitiation, it most assuredly can never sink low enough to count it a salvation that pains are simply bought off by pains, in the close exchange of expiation.

I make this explicit renouncement of expiation with less satisfaction, that so many disciples appear to be under a partly superstitious impression of its immense practical value. They look upon it as the central truth about which genuinely christian experience must revolve. They conceive a certain mysterious fitness in it to the needs of the conscience, alleging that the conscience is no casuist, deals in no refine-

<small>No interest of character in expiation.</small>

ments, questions never about the delicate distinctions, never waits to have the gospel smooth itself out in the psychologic proprieties; wanting, therefore, never any thing so much as a good square paying in of pains for pains, penalties suffered for penalties deserved. Let there be no winnowing out of substance and power by our explanations. Let the emancipation be as under the Roman law, when a slave is made free by a blow on his head. No matter if questions rise and doubts remain, they come from the head; let the head take care of them, and let the conscience be going its way sheltered by God's peace. Many teachers magnify expiation thus under an appeal of ignorance. They acknowledge that it does not stand well in speculation, and that many reasons are lifted up in mutiny against it. Still it is the simple gospel they think, because it makes good the conscience; for the conscience having no philosophy, can be pacified only by a way of settlement that transcends philosophy, and ignores all casuistries. It has, at any rate, they say, the necessary ring; for which reason the strongest, most pronounced ideas of expiation are necessary to the best effects in christian living. For self is thus cut off, and self-endeavor and all the legalities of duty. Speculation is given up; for when expiation is taken for the religion, there is no room for speculation left. And what shall we look for but to see the simple man be simply good and righteous? for the reason that he is taken away from all doubting and even opinion.

Now that such impressions are groundless I most confidently believe, and also think observation will show. Indeed, I will venture the assertion that the most intensely expiational form of christianity, instead of being most robust and steadfast, is poorest in the general, most unreliable, most frequently immoral. And that for the almost necessary reason, that it expects to have salvation by a coarse commercial transaction in the exchange of pains. Are not the punishments all made up? is not the law quite satisfied? What shall we do then but let go concern, and plunge ourselves in the unanalyzed, unfiltered, waters of salvation? Why so delicate in making critically nice distinctions of things in our approach to God, when he expiates our sins by the death of his Son, without caring to do it in a way that meets our dainty feelings and convictions. No! it is an awful mistake, to speak in this coarse way of clearing the conscience. Such kind of uncaring peace will be only a dry-rot in the conscience, absolving it from duty instead of sin, and preparing the man to be religiously and, as it were, devoutly irresponsible. Looseness and unthinkingness are themselves disorder begun, and will run to worse and worse disorder as they proceed. Let us know in whom we believe, what he has done, what his atoning is, how he could and did, and how he could not and did not, become our sacrifice. Let us count our salvation a matter high enough and rich enough to be studied, searched out, nicely discriminated. No faith in the gross, that makes a fetich of the cross, is going to stand proof. The disciple will become distinctly, nobly christian only when he takes the propitiation as it is offered, and lives by faith in it, as the tide-flow of God's free forgiveness.

CHAPTER II.

LAW AND COMMANDMENT.

The forgiveness of sins, already considered in the chapter on Forgiveness and Propitiation, is a purely personal matter, in which the Fatherhood love and feeling and the offended holiness of God are concerned. The proceeding here is intelligible and simple, because the forgiveness in question is to be a strictly Personal Settlement, that and that only. Then comes the farther question of the impersonal wrongs of law, and their Legal Settlement. All wrongs, taken as personal offenses, <small>The Legal Settlement.</small> are yet violations also of law, and forgiveness being personal has no power, of course, to right the injuries of broken law. The law, too, being impersonal can not of course forgive any thing itself; or any way compound its own wrong; neither is it conceivable that God, as the administrator of law, has any power to annul the fact of such wrong, or the fact of a damage done by it to the law. Forgiveness, we thus find, puts a man personally right with God, but it does not put him right with law, and it is not easy to see that any thing can. The retributive consequences of violated law are running still in his nature; only so far reduced as the moral disorders of his nature are rectified, and the blight of his transgressions removed by the health-restoring efficacy of the regeneration. Made partly or completely whole, he will be partly or completely clear of the penal effects of the law, never till then. At this single point and so far, forgiveness has to do with law, and law with forgiveness, and I really do not see that they have a single point of contact any where else; except as the law continues to press the enforcement of a life that can fitly be forgiven.

And yet we appear to be assuming always, in this matter of atonement, that a principal concern of the salvation is to mend up, or somehow rehabilitate the law, when the indulgences of forgiveness are allowed; and especially to find how the standing offer of forgiveness can be proclaimed without consequent damage to its integrity. We assume, as if any thing could satisfy a law but simply and eternally to keep it, that the law broken by transgression must be satis-

Satisfaction of the law. fied. Not satisfied by obedience, it must be by punishment; not satisfied by the punishment of the wrong doer, it must be by the punishment of a substitute; not by the punishment of a substitute in legal measure, it must be by some governmental equivalent in the expression of suffering, that will mend the public honor of the law and keep it good. Meantime, as regards this matter of satisfying law, it is a very great question whether enduring the penalty of transgression in full measure satisfies it; for the felon who has served the time of his sentence completely out, is really no more approved by the law than he was before. He is not, in fact, approved at all and never can be till he makes a new character, and conquers to himself a new approbation. Still we go on con-   *Inventions and* triving theologic ways of satisfying   *devices.* God's law, till, by one or another mode of getting its penalties made up, we think it is done. We propose substitutions for penalty, and compensations for penalty, and transferable merits provided, and righteousnesses made up to even accounts, and sins carried over by transfer to another, and sins accepted for the sinner in the liabilities of his guilt, with justice executed upon the guilt thus responsibly taken. Using these for theologic counters, we go on working out computations of atonement, and showing how it is that Christ is able to unlock the gates of law and bring transgressors through, without damage to its integrity. To any christian believer the story ought to be a very sad one; for the schemes built on these vocables are, of course, not more genuine than they. I will not charge that they are an altogether spurious brood, but the artificial look they carry is conspicuous. And their look is the more suspicious that they take on scripture semblances without any scripture meanings—save as we distinguish dimly the inverted images a great way off. Their intellectual figure, too, is a dismal sign for their supposed affinity with the gospel; for they do not present a possible idea, but always instead an impossible. On the whole, there is an aspect of discouragement really forbidding in all these endeavors, turning on the satisfaction of law or the satisfaction of penalty. We all the while suspect some juggle of theologic art in the processes themselves. As if the law were to be somehow gotten out of the way, without fulfillment—contrary to Christ's own word when he declares, in solemn protestation to the world, that he is not come to destroy the law but to fulfill it. "For verily I say unto you, Till heaven and earth pass, one jot or one tittle shall in no wise pass from the law, till all be fulfilled."* In the verse previous it is literally *to* "*fulfill*," but here it is, "*be come to pass*"—as if some thought of futurition were in mind, and as if he felt himself ordained to help on the law, and see it bring its crowning ideas to pass. A very different matter from that satisfying of the law which shows a process provided, by the counsel of heaven, for getting its penalties out of the innocent instead of the guilty! The true Legal Fulfillment, which is the present object of our inquiry, is certainly not here. It will begin, as to its ruling idea, where Legal Obedience begins; that is in keeping and fulfilling the law; for the law, as we shall see, does not drop us the moment we transgress, but it comes on after us, like a faithful schoolmaster, joining its discipline with the grace of the cross and the grace of the Spirit, as

---

* Matthew v, 17-18.

truly concerned as they to gather us back into liberty.

I can not undertake, at this point, to state, in a formal way, the doctrine I am going to advance, for that is not yet possible. I shall be obliged, instead, to throw myself on the patience of my readers, and ask them to go along with me, stage by stage, till I have opened the subject far enough to make it possible. I will then set forth a general proposition that will cover the whole ground of the chapter.

I.

I know not any better point where to open the proposed discussion, than where, at a certain favoring hour, it seemed to be first opened to me. Were it not a fact *(Begin at Christ and his commandments.)* so thoroughly sealed by our dull repetitions, I think it would certainly be most remarkable, that the man Jesus—call him divine, or simply human, for outwardly, at least, he is but a man—should so often and boldly insist on "the keeping of his commandments," as the standard test of his disciples. The wonder is too, that he does it so much as a matter of course! And what shall we say of it?—that this humble, uneducated man, this peasant going as a foot passenger through the world, this wise man who is not a philosopher, this king without royalty or family, whom nobody has chosen, and whom fortune has not put in a condition to secure him shelter for his head, whose mission is to suffer, and who only proposes to draw adherents by the yielding up of his life; that he, a man so lowly and gentle, should put it on mankind to "keep his commandments"—is it not a fact most remarkable in itself, and one that may fitly arrest our attention? Plainly it is either a good deal more, or a great deal less than what we make of it. And have we no reason to suspect that we are losing immensely in our outfit of Christian ideas, by the very great inadequacy of our teaching at this point? Perhaps we miss any fit impression of it, by referring the Saviour's injunction mentally to his deific nature, counting it only a matter of course that he should sometimes speak out of his deific consciousness? And we have a way of doing this so often, to magnify his condescensions and the winning tenderness of his self-sacrificing devotion, that we scarcely leave him any thing at all, but in deific right. We call him Master, indeed, as a man, but when he comes to put his Masterhood on us, requiring us to keep his commandments, we do not quite imagine that he does it simply as a man; he is only bidding us acknowledge his superior right and take the good injunction he is able to give, in the certainly deific authority by which he gives it. No, he speaks as the man that came down from heaven; and there is no great master of philosophy that ever undertook such authority, or that men would ever acknowledge for one moment in doing it. Neither Socrates, nor Plato, nor Bacon, nor Kant,

Who is he, to command the world?

ever thought of putting his commandment on the world, or of bringing his followers, in the test of their character, to the keeping of his commandments. But Jesus does it with no token of misgiving. And he does it evidently in the emphasis expected to be felt and the impression to be made, by his own transcendent personality. He glows, he beams, he rises in stature and becomes a half transfigured form, by the lifted consciousness he is in. That we are going to understand him in these commandments as simply putting us on keeping God's requirements, he plainly does not even imagine.

Our attention then is here called to the Commandments Christ will have us keep as our standard, and to the Law of God before enacted to be our standard; especially to what they are in their mutual relations to each other. And it <small>General statement.</small> may serve to make our way more intelligible, if we set up beforehand the point on which we shall be moving; viz., that what is called the law is to be consummated, brought to pass, fulfilled, in Christ's commandments. The law, by itself, makes nothing in us answer to its own high intentions, and is never expected, simply as law, to become a footing of salvation. But it is to make a beginning of moral impression, or enforced obligation, afterwards to be consummated in the state of allegiance to Christ, and the keeping of his commandments; where the old enforcements are substituted largely by a service in liberty; where, in fact, a new character is born, answering both to the law and the commandments by which the law was to be fulfilled. It is not to be said that the law is satisfied as being accurately kept—the satisfaction idea has no place here, unless it be understood as being satisfied in that it comes at last to be fulfilled. This brief statement will suffice to indicate beforehand the doctrine I am going to undertake, and it will be more fully and explicitly discovered, in the future progress of my argument.

The two words *law* and *commandment*—*nomos* and *entolē*—will settle into place most easily in our exposition, if we consider them; I., Separately, in what they signify apart from each other; II., In their offices and uses; and then; III., In their mutual relations to each other. Only I desire at this early stage of the inquiry to place it as distinctly as possible before the observation of my reader that I do not represent, and do not in fact believe that the two words *nomos* and *entolē* uniformly hold in the scripture the precise relative significance given them in the exposition that follows. They vary, sometimes one falling very nearly into the sense of the other, so that discrimination is lost. And sometimes they even seem to cross over and make an exchange of meaning. Still a very close insertion of the critical knife will generally uncover some aspect of reason for the fluctuations discovered. But it must be enough for my present purpose, as I think it will be allowed, that the two words commonly and almost always in the New Testament, stand in the relative significance I have given them. And this will be the more readily conceded, that I do not use them so much for authority as for convenience; though I do most certainly discover in them just the complexions of meaning that make them convenient for my uses. I think also it will be agreed that I subject them to no violence. We proceed then to inquire—

I. What the two terms signify taken separately. In what is called the law, we have, at the foundation, that great distinction of our moral nature, which makes us moral beings by a property inherent; viz., the eternal, absolute, self-asserting idea of right; that which is the law before government, and a law to God in composing his government, as truly as to us, after it is composed; that in which we become a law to ourselves, showing the work of the law written on our hearts. And then we have superadded to this, for its more specific application, or carrying out into practice, statutes instituted by God in a way of positive enactment, appointing what we are to do, or not to do, for the due fulfillment of the aforesaid absolute, all-inclusive law. These positive word-statutes are also themselves enlarged and farther expounded, in turn, by the moral legislations of the Scripture, and by the common law of society; that is by custom, by legal definition, by refinements of æsthetic perception, as well as by the drill practice of all the functional experiences. By these two concurrent methods, divine legislation and the custom of society, we obtain a moral code more or less complete; that, for example, of the ten commandments, and that which is ethically developed about them and separately from them. And then, besides, we have additions in the Mosaic code, of liturgical law not moral, by which observances are enjoined that are designed to help the religious worship of the age then present, and to prepare a language of sacrifice for the future uses of the great salvation afterwards to be completed in the sacrifice of Christ—a kind of forecasting and provisional legislation, whose uses, over and above the present uses of the altar worship, could not appear for a long time to come, but when they should arrive would be "fulfillments" properly so called. Probably this word "*fulfill*" was used by the Saviour in mental reference, partly, to the futuritions of the law in this liturgical department.

In this description then we have the law [the *nomos*]; a rigidly unpersonal, abstract, statutory code of conduct, based in the everlasting, inherent, moral imperative, that underlies it, and gives authority both to the Supreme Legislator and his legislations. It is the law before government, and then by government; enforced by sanctions self-pronounced, and then by sanctions also that are legally prescribed. On the whole we shall probably understand what the law is, most comprehensively and most exactly, if we take the Saviour's own summation of it; for this, it will be seen, covers in fact all we have said both of its absolute right and its practical necessity. "Thou shalt love the Lord thy God, with all thy heart, and with all thy soul, and with all thy strength, and with all thy mind, and thy neighbor as thyself." For if we call this God's consummate act of legislation, it still was law, absolute, in a sense, before all legislation.

Let us next consider what is meant by the commandment [*entolē*], that which Christ understands when he enjoins the keeping of his commandments, and gives to be the test henceforth of true discipleship. Any one can see that the word commandment is generally a less statutory, less tabulated, and more flexibly personal word than the word law. As used by Christ, it commands in the sense of enjoining, and enjoins in the sense of a personal authority, and assumes to be a personal authority, by reason of the qualities embodied, and offices performed, in his ministry. It covers just all that is commended to man's feeling and conscience by his life and death. Sometimes he uses the term "words" as the synonym of "commandments," requiring us to keep his words and have them abiding in us. On a certain occasion he sums up all his claims of homage and obedience under the word yoke—"Take my yoke upon you and learn of me." The yoke is a symbol even of brute subjection, and is applied for that reason to nations going under captivity. But he softens the term by his most tender assurances—" for I am meek and lowly in heart, and ye shall find rest to your souls."* That is, "coming

margin: The commandment.

---

* Matthew xi, 28–30.

under me and my commandments, and learning of me, ye shall no longer be galled as by living only under law, but ye shall be filled with all comfort and entered into liberty and rest." His meaning is the same when he calls himself "the way:" for the commandment is no assertion of authority simply, like the law, but a gently guiding power for the trust of erring souls. Again, it is another conception of his commandment that he is in the world as a person to be followed; a person who types all goodness and draws all loving homages into his own likeness. He does not say in the imperative, as the law does, "follow or die," but he says, "whosoever doth not follow, forsaking all to do it, can not, as in liberty, be my disciple." Sometimes he emphasizes his commandment, and draws it to a closer point of homage, by insisting on that completeness of sacrifice which takes up even the cross to be with him. "He that loveth father or mother more than me is not worthy of me, and he that loveth son or daughter more than me is not worthy of me; and he that taketh not his cross and followeth after me is not worthy of me." He asserts himself in like manner before Pilate as the king of truth and so the commander of the world, saying, "every one that is of the truth heareth my voice."

He does not mean by his commandment then, or

<small>The commandment unlegal.</small> the keeping of his commandments, that he is here to put us under syllables and the statutory dictations of law, such as by their

exactness and thunderous majesty, made even Moses "exceedingly fear and quake," but he is here as personal commandment, to impress what a person may, and be what a person can, of supreme light and all-transforming benignity. So that what he insists upon, in the keeping of his commandments, does not mean a cringing and timorous observance, a bondage of scruple and servile abasement, but a keeping in dear homages that count their object precious—even as a miser keeps his money, or the mother keeps her child, or a patriot his country. How very different a matter is that grudging, slavish way of keeping the commandments, that is contriving always how to pass the test, by being exactly up and even with them. The true keeping is different, that of a body guard, that which is free as love is, not that which is in bonds looking after the jot and tittle because it must. It is the noble form of duty, which thinks not of what is to be feared, but of what is treasure to be lovingly guarded. And it is here, at this point, that the Saviour's test displays the consummate worth and glory of a character, in him, complete.

I ought, perhaps, in so many specifications of what is meant by the commandment, to name the equivalent Paul gives for it, and so lovingly commends as if it were a kind of gospel-way before the gospel, viz., the dispensation called Promise;* that which came to Abraham to be taken hold of by his faith; that which the law, *The Promise.*

---
* Gal. iii, 14–19.

coming four hundred years after, could not annul, or make of none effect; that which went with all good men before the law, according to their faith, and was their commandment, unpronounced but inwardly felt, even down to the incarnate appearing. And then Christ himself, in his commandment, undertakes to keep good the liberty of the promise, and guide his people on by inspirations from his own manifested love and sacrifice.

And yet I must not omit to cite a still better exposition by a still higher authority; that is, by Christ himself. In one of his farewell discourses, reported by John,* he dwells at large on the subject, using, within a very few verses, the terms command, commandment, and commandments. He begins by comparing their keeping of his commandments with his own keeping of the Father's, the result of which will be that they abide in his love even as he in the Father's. Of course he does not mean that in the Father's commandments he is under any legal relation, or any bonds of penalty; such an idea would be altogether abhorrent. As little does he mean the like, when he puts them to the keeping of his own. The state effected will be in both cases the same, an abiding in love—he in the Father's, they in his. He goes on further to say that he looks to the relation that will be established, as a relation of simple friendship, in which they will be governed by no dictation,

Christ expounds the commandments himself.

---

* John xv, 10–15.

but simply as a friend governs a friend. Ye are my friends if ye do whatsoever I command you. Henceforth I call you not servants, as I may have sometimes seemed to do before—ye are not my bondmen, nor my hirelings, nor my servitors or domestics—but I have called you friends, intending therein to signify a state of dearest privity, in which you are let into my sympathies, and ends, and counsels, far enough to be able to command yourselves—even as Christ was in the counsel of the Father without any statutory direction. How sublime and blessed the relationship!

II. The offices and uses of the law and the commandment. And here we shall see, at a glance, that the law, by itself, is not expected or intended to result in any complete form of personal virtue or character. It is to make a beginning in the level of constrained motive, using intimidations for the enforcement of principles, hammering in thus, or grinding in as it were, certain first impressions and first obligations necessary to character, as being its previous conditions. More exactly still it has for its office, to unfold the moral sense, and break the confidence of guilt, by revealing the dangers of disobedience. It ordains no fruitional, but a frictional experience rather, such as puts the subject writhing in condemnations, and conscious bondages, and apprehensions of evil to come. Accepted for its excellence, it would be life, and this it was designed

Offices and uses.

to be, if only it could, but though it is ordained for life, it is found to be unto death. But the death is to be, in fact, a main element of its value. For the subject, slain by the law, is yet in a training under it that is a highway opening into life. In one view it exasperates all the dispositions, working thus disorder, discord, discouragement, and even a kind of disability, which still it is hoped may turn to benefit by the complete self-forsaking it prepares. Considered as ordained before transgression it is right, because it asserts a claim to homage that puts the soul, when accepted, on the footing of society with God, and blessedness in his favor. And yet, considering the inexperience and crudity of that state, it could not be expected to issue in any such way, save as it issued first in a state of downfall and moral disaster, to be afterwards mended by a recovery. "If there had been a law given which could have given life," says Paul, intimating his conviction of the impossibility; but it could have a real and powerful use, he thinks, when "added because of transgressions," that is to unfold the consciousness of transgression after the fact, and put the malefactor sighing for deliverance.

So far the law has no value save as a first stage of discipline, to be followed by another that will bring on the discipline to a result that is complete. It is, and is declared to be "the ministration of death," "the letter that killeth," and it is only "the ministration of righteousness," "the spirit that giveth life," that can make it better than a simply disastrous appointment.

What we call the law of God then, and what the theologians have been magnifying with so great homage and almost idolatry, is not, after all, as we here discover, a perfect institute in itself, and was never meant to be. It has an inevitable, necessary imperfection, open to all discovery. (1.) That it proposes to work only by penal enforcements, making their appeal to self-interested motive and that only, and holding every subject, as far as it goes, fast down upon self-consideration; so that acting by itself alone it will never bring the subject on to a way of duty freely chosen for its own sake. (2.) That it works for the most part, and must, by negative statutes that forbid, and not by positive that command. Thus, taking for example the ten commandments, we find them just where all low-grounded evil minds are wont to pitch their moralities; saying, "thou shalt not," "thou shalt not," in their every article save the fifth. There was, of course, no training into life, under these mere negatives. If they were able to keep the low-bred sinners of Israel back from being as bad as they otherwise might be, and level them up to a condition of society politically tolerable, it was all that could be expected, though here and there some one, taken by the Spirit, might be carried by, into something higher. If they undertook to keep the whole table of statute, in a way of puncti-

The law no perfect institute.

The law is negative mostly.

lious observance, it would only make them legalists, and chain them down to that mere statute-keeping kind of virtue. The precise difficulty we have here with the law is, in fact, that it was only as good and high as it could be; for the people of that first age could not even take the sense of any thing above their mental range. Thus Ezekiel, the prophet, tells the people expressly that "God gave them statutes not good,"* or the best, probably because they were too low in their perceptions to be commanded by any thing better. (3.) It is another large sub-traction from the *nomos* or the statute-mode of impersonal, tabulated rule, that it brings no inspirations, and yokes the subject to God by no faith climbing into the sense of his friendship. If there were no God back of the law, the case would not be different, save that his idea, coming in by way of authority, adds more stringency to the rules enforced. What then is more forlorn to think of, than that such a creature as man, made to be filled with deific inspirations, and wafted onward in the everlasting liberties of the righteousness of God, is shut down thus under a law-state which provides no stimulations, or visitations of life, more ennobling than mere authority and fear? I say these things, observe, in no way of complaint. The law is just as good as it can be, doing just all for the subject in the way of legal benefit that it can. There is no possible repair of the deficit, but the bringing

<small>No great inspiration.</small>

---

* Ezekiel xx, 25.

in of a better hope. (4.) A mere law regimen is of necessity in scant measure, holding the principal ideas of *love* and *right* in a short way that does not measure them by God's measures, but by the measures of natural thought in men and the natural standards of society. God's intentions in the law are scanted, of course, by no such measures, but the moral ideas of men will be, till they are taken up out of the law and above it, by the second stage of discipline to be provided in the commandment.

<small>Stunted by want of perception.</small>

Passing onward now to this second stage, we have it as our next point to consider the offices and uses of the commandment Christ is giving us to keep as our new standard. And here we are to notice, first, the enlarged spread of the standard. Under the terms *love* and *righteousness* Christ goes a full day's journey, so to speak, beyond the law as held in men's thoughts, opening a vast province of culture, where the evangelic riches and liberties are gloriously enlarged and widened in their flow. According to the merely human, or legally humanized notions, love means only love to our neighbor, on the footing of our fellow nature. The word of Christ goes farther—" But I say unto you love your enemies, bless them that curse you, do good to them that hate you, and pray for them that despitefully use you and persecute you." The law of natural society is, love the lovely, and

<small>Offices and uses of the commandment.</small>

the law of God conceived under that restriction amounts to scarcely more than a law of good society.

<small>Love.</small> But Christ proposes a nobler and more sovereign love—love the unlovely, the base, the wicked, the hateful, the disgustful—instituting thus a new divine order of love in sacrifice, and cost, and patience. This is the love that goes under, and up through evil, and regenerates all it touches; heaving, as it were, every mountain of incumbrance that sin has piled on the world. So again

<small>Righteousness.</small> there is a righteousness in Christ's view that the Scribes and Pharisees had not under the law in their most superstitious observance of it, and scarcely better I fear is our half-commercial righteousness, where we assume that right means only what is fair, equitable, or just. To Christ there is no right or righteousness that does not go a long way farther. No man is in the right, or up to the right, who is not ready for sacrifice and the enduring of cost for the ill-deserving. And hence it is that our Great Master is pronounced, as it were, on discovery to the world—" Jesus Christ the righteous" —and the definite article is prefixed, to challenge for him his pre-eminent distinction. Hence, also, that other pronouncement not less remarkable, " faithful and righteous—[not just, but righteous] to forgive us our sins;" as if God would not think himself completely righteous in his Son, were there any utmost sacrifice and cost he could not undergo for the forgiveness of sins.

And what a chapter is opened for us here, in these words *love* and *right*, as they will henceforth be represented in the life of Christ by commandment. How far on do they reach beyond the measures of the merely legal code. In this legal code we live, as it were, outside of God, under the statute, shrunken up, and shriveled by the stringency of mere penal enforcement. Here, in the commandment, we live inside, where we range in glorious enlargement by God's measures, and are no more scanted in love and right by the meager notions, whether of Pharisees or ethical professors.

Secondly, there is, I think, sufficient distinctness in the fact to require some distinct notice of it, that we not only come abroad here into wider and more enriched ways of excellence, but that we have our discipline by a different and more genial method. We leave the mere *Leaving the law.* tabulated, impersonal, statutory way of rule, and pass out into a way of commandment that is personal, and is, in fact, the rounded, all-containing sway of personality itself. In simply being what it is, it is commandment, and word, and way, and yoke, made easy; for it is the living and dying Christ in whom all the authorities and captivating majesties of good are contained. The intimidations are gone by, at least for the time. The word is a word of Christly inspiration—take my yoke, take up my cross, walk in my way, as I live, live with me, as I die, be joined to me in death. Our life code is given in the person of

Jesus, and in that *living book* gets authority to be our commandment. And it is a way of commandment that leaves us free, nay that makes us free. Legal obedience is gone by forever. Impulse, inspiration, duties that are meat and drink—these are the tide-sweep of the new life quickened in us. The Son makes us free, and therefore we are free indeed. The Spirit goes with the word and commandment, as it does not with the law, wafting us onward, and where the Spirit of the Lord is there is liberty. Nay the law itself, if we use that word, being in us no more by enforcement, is become the perfect law of liberty. And so the result is that when we are engaged to keep the commandment of Jesus, we have it keeping us, floating us on, tiding us in upon the divine fullness where we rest.

There is yet a third consideration that must not be omitted; viz., that the commandment differs from the law as being offered to faith. The law is apprehended, or expected to be, only as all statutes are; that is by ocular inspection, audible pronouncement, and other like natural ways of cognition. But the Christ-law, or commandment, is given to faith, even as Christ himself is, for in fact it is himself in the scope of its ideas and resulting obligations. It has no penal sanctions whatever, but speaking directly to faith it offers promise, always promise, working thus by comforts, inspirations, openings upwards into God. In this way, making its appeal to faith, it enlarges, lifts, kindles with energy such as belongs to the Mighty Great One whose commandment and way of life it has chosen. Full account is made in this way of the fact that faith is the summit faculty and upper sense of the mind; that by which all greatest, highest things enter into mortals. Looking in here from afar over the battlements into the eternal city, it is as if the word of faith had taken us up thither. We enter, as it were beforehand, by a kind of anticipative apprehension, or visional beatitude. But the law could not begin at faith. What could it say addressing faith? Even the God of the law must take the prudential footing in it, setting in authority by enforcements of fear, and causing sins to wince by their bondages and dreaded wages. Faith gets no chance till after another chapter is opened, where some new grace of life is given to be accepted, or offered to be believed in. The good God coming in mercy and sacrifice to save—he only signals to faith. But if the law were to say believe, setting up statutes for it in penalty, there would certainly be a very wide chasm between that kind of artillery and the believing required.

III. We come now to the third and last point in our proposed explication; viz., the relation of the Law and the Commandment to each other. *The relations of the two.* They have a common object, there is to be no doubt of that; viz., to establish right and finish up a truly ennobled character of deific righteousness in mankind. But they never did it, or proposed to do it, by either, in its own separate agency. In the first place, the law, it is agreed, makes no righteousness of its own. Indeed, it is even declared to be the letter that killeth —ordained unto life, but found to be unto death. I think too we can see beforehand, that any table of statute working by itself, and forcing on virtues by motives in the nature of retribution, must bring failure and precipitation; though even that may become the necessary footing of a new second-stage movement forward. Be it so, still they are both in line together, moving, each in its way, on the common interest of character. By one is the knowledge of sin, by the other the deliverance from it; and the knowledge being necessary to the deliverance, has a certain common value with it. We shall discover thus, as regards the relative action of the two great factors, law and commandment, that the law is just as necessary to the result as the commandment, and that the latter, taken by itself, can do as little as the law by itself. The expectation was, and is, that a beginning made under the latter and the legal intimidations, will stamp in such imprints of authority and obligation, and raise such storms of disorder and wild remorse within, when they are violated, that the subject, driven out of all confidence in himself, will be casting about for almost any deliverance from the dreadful precipitation that is thrusting him down. Whereupon it is the plan to bring him out and up by his faith in the commandment, or second stage of discipline, into a state of new-born life. So that, between the two, and by one as truly as the other, the great final end of liberty and holy character will be consummated. If we say fulfilled, we mean the same thing; for the law, when even already broken, is to be fulfilled in the commandment as truly and totally as if it had never been broken; perhaps the more completely fulfilled that, after the breach, exasperated longings, and heart-sinking bondages, and writhings of remorse, will have created a hell in the mind, that is to be the eternal possibility of juster apprehensions and vaster yearnings; such as will be spanning forever the chasm that the breach has made.

It needs also to be noted, as regards the two great factors, law and commandment, that one is a factor in nature and among natural causes, and the other supernatural. *One a factor in nature, the other supernatural.* The apostle shows them working both together—the weakness of one and the relative might of the other. "For what the law could not do, in that it was weak through the flesh"—that is through the mere constitution-life in which both law and penalty are to get their pronouncement—"God sending his own Son in the likeness of sinful flesh, condemned sin in the flesh, that the righteousness of the law might be fulfilled in us, who walk not after the flesh, but after the Spirit." Every thing is weak on the footing of law, but every thing begun there triumphs in the supernatural vigor of the Spirit; for the commandment, as being spirit and truth, is supernatural vigor itself. Penal causations are the power in the one, and it is a dreadful power; supernatural ministrations, separating the guilty from their hidden poisons and their low-bred disabilities, are the power in the other. Natural causes, appointed to avenge the law, suffer no violence or displacement by the supernatural grace, but this latter visitation, quickening good in the man and the man to good, in a manner of silent sovereignty, makes the natural causes slacken their hold on him and let him forth made whole and free.

The law, it is important to add, is in this view never abolished or annulled by the commandment, though it is a common way of the evangelic teaching to very nearly say it. Some may think it is even said by the scripture; as where it is declared, "For there is verily a disannulling of the commandment going before, for the weakness and unprofitableness thereof; for the law made nothing perfect, but the bringing in of a better hope did."* But this is not said of the moral-law table, as will be seen at a glance by reference to the passage, but of the ceremonial law, and specially of the priesthood; which was only a lighter and very subordinate part of the law, that was added, in fact, to be taken away. There is indeed a single passage, it must be allowed, where the law side of the double ministration we are discussing is spoken of as being done away—"For if that which is done away was glorious, much more that which remaineth is glorious."† But the real fact

Law never abolished.

---

* Heb. vii, 18–19. † 2 Cor. iii, 11.

here intended is, beyond a question, that the new free life of the commandment takes away the subject from the law, and not the law from the subject. Just as the same apostle says, "Ye are become dead to the law by the body of Christ."* He does not say for the law is become dead to you, but ye are become dead to the law. And yet in still another place he does even speak of the law itself as dead. "But now we are delivered from the law, that being dead wherein we were held, that we should serve in newness of spirit and not in the oldness of the letter."† Yet even here he plainly enough does not mean that the law is abrogated and gone, in that sense dead, but only that, in practical living, we go over from the old to the new, and have our central homage there. Plainly enough the law of God never can be taken away from any world or creature; for with it, in close company, goes abroad all the conserving principle, moral and physical, in which God's kingdom stands.

A thousand crosses, ransoms, atonements, would leave it exactly where it was. The taking away of sin was possible, but no taking away of the law. The sacrifice of Calvary itself, set against the law, would have had as little effect on it as upon the principles of Euclid. Therefore we must never allow to be slid into our secret apprehension, back of thought, any most latent feeling that God is at work in his Son to mend, or mitigate, or get us by, the law. It is whole as it ever was. Broken oft, as in

---

* Romans vii, 4. † Romans vii, 6.

figure, it is yet not flawed; condemning still and always every thing in principle it has condemned; certain to outlast the world, even as it lived before the world in the eternal bosom of God.*

II.

This very specific and scriptural exposition of the two great factors, the commandment and the law, and their relative work and office, is a gathering up of material, it will be understood, for the great Legal Settlement or Consummation which is the proposed subject of our inquiry.

What this exposition is for.

But we are not yet ready to use this material to the best advantage, and can not be till we have gone over another field not scriptural, and brought in the rich fund of matters there supplied for our help. Knowing, as we all do, that God's way, in casting the molds of things, is to show us first what is natural, and afterwards what is spiritual, as it may be signified thereby; to show us things in human life and society set to represent, by analogic correspondences, things of the Spirit and things Celestial, making always the lower to be interpreters of the higher—men's forgivenesses, of God's forgivenesses—the family, of God's great Fatherhood—the state, of God's infinite kingdom—knowing this, I say, it is the more remarkable that we miss observing the numerous analogies of law and gospel continually crowded upon us in our natural and earthly state. It can not be that these low-ranging, sub-atoning ways of discipline, all beginning

---

* Note 3.

with law and meant to be issued in liberty, have no important lessons to give us in the field of religion. Let me call attention to a few of the numerous examples.

I begin with the training of childhood, where the two factors, authority and love, penal constraint and a naturally vicarious tenderness in the mother, work together, as the law and commandment, making up the compound discipline that is to establish the obedience of the child. She goes to her charge thus, in the endeavor to make her child the man he should be. But the restive boy, just passing out of infancy, wonders that he must be so continually hampered by restrictions. He loses temper once an hour, stands looking doggedly down when commanded, and shakes off the hand that is kindly put upon him. A little farther on he debates every thing, grows irascible and stormy that he can not have his own way, when he knows so well himself exactly what he wants! Which is the most vexatious, the doing required of him, or the doing forbidden him, it may be difficult to say; enough that he is twisting all the while in one sort of annoyance or the other. Of course there is a difference of temperament in children, and a great many mothers are indiscreet in the over-multiplication of things forbidden. Still, where the administration is most considerate and most tenderly faithful, there will often be stormy scenes of impatience, and sometimes punishment will be unavoidable. Old enough to sympathize with

Mother and child.

himself, and galled, as he thinks, by real chains, his very day's life becomes a pain; is there no relief? But there comes along by and by, later than we should expect, and late enough to cost his mother hours of great anxiety, a stray thought in a different key. Perhaps it is suggested by what has been observed in some other family, where a comrade child is glad and bright in the sunshine of his mother's control. Now begins revision at the question, not unlikely, is my mother less good than his? is her control less faithfully meant? might I not as well be happy and sunny myself? And so the result is that the boy who, at eight years of age, was tearing himself against every point of maternal restriction, will finally, at thirty, obey every softest wish of his mother as if it were an edict, and will even catch it by anticipation before it is expressed. Probably the old struggles of his childhood, and the fight of impatience under his mother's law, are so far gone by now as scarcely to be remembered. And yet that rule stays by him still, deep down, central, silent, and commanding, as it were, in the very homages of his grown up sonship. The fears are gone out, the discipline is over, all the frictions by which she was rubbing in the moral of her authority, are spent, but her motherly right is even the more decisively asserted now that it makes no self-assertion at all. This remarkable change is often noticed, and is generally ascribed, I think, to the habit principle. But habit only fastens what has been the way of practice.

The man therefore ought to be only more doggedly set in his opposition to rule and authority, because of the impatience of his childhood. He would be, if he had not somehow found his way out into the obedience of liberty. That transition clearly was not made by habit, but the habit he is now in, if we call it by that name, was rather begun itself at the transition. The spontaneous homage he now pays to his mother is pure liberty, and has no legal quality whatever, save that her law is tacitly centered in him and he knows it not.

From the family we pass to the school. The behavior here is prescribed by rule, the hours and times are fixed, the lessons are appointed. *The school discipline.* Play meantime is held in embargo, and idleness put under spur. And the result is very commonly that the whole affair is distasteful—a bondage, a dreariness—making the books and prescribed lessons a drug. And the very reason is that knowledge has now to be sought by law before it is wanted by appetite. Every thing goes on by statute, and of course drags heavily. And so it will be, till some grand mind-loving soul comes out in the Master, making study, Arnold-wise, of the boy, to find what is in him and put him in his line of promise. The result is now that a fire is kindled and a new capacity is born. Ceasing to be a drudge, he now begins to hunger after knowledge itself, set on by devotion to study for its own sake, as he once could not think it possible to be. Sometimes this enthusiasm gets kindled very late. But after the fire once begins to blaze, there will not be hours enough in day and night together, to satisfy the appetite engaged. The school is now gone by, we say, the old day of fixed lessons and fixed hours, and compelled digging at the books—all the legal ways of the drill—are spent, and yet we shall come much nearer to the true conception, if we say they are all fulfilled substantially now in the self-prompted endeavor and free play of liberty. Knowledge is now desired and study pursued for its own sake—just what the old law drill of the lessons was for, but could not bring to pass, till the inspirations came, and then the work was done.

Turning in still another direction, we encounter
Labor and the the institute of labor, organized from
curse. the beginning by a law that undertakes
the training of men correctively towards ways of industry, and reformatively out of ways of self-indulgence, which is the bane of all responsibility and character. There is no law more truly beneficent. We call it the law of the curse, and rightly, but it is none the less truly beneficent on that account. Muscular toil or labor is naturally irksome to men, and the sweat of the brow is no popular institution. All the worse when compelled by the grinding stress of necessity. Any law of work, driven home by that kind of enforcement, is justly called a curse. But cursed as the ground is, and cursed as the toil, it is yet a right good curse, as all workers discover, when

they find their way on, through the compulsions of work, into the liberties. When the sense of skill is waked and the sense of creatorship, when a home is endowed and the acres in culture smile their glad acknowledgment, when children arrive and the little patrons of the cradle and the table look their blessing, the drudgery, that was, becomes a privilege; the industry, a song. The worker's greatest difficulty now is to set himself limits and take the needed rest. To him now there is no curse in labor. He scarcely sees, perhaps stoutly denies, the world-blight of transgression itself. It is even as if that world-blight law were taken clean away; so grandly is it fulfilled and fulfilling, as regards the moral intent of it, in the joyous and free industries that are become the life of his life—drudgeries all in their law-state, now become the state of play.

Again, we meet another strangely impressive example in the army discipline. It begins with a code of rules or camp orders, precise, inflexible, unconditionally severe. The problem of the discipline is first of all to make the soldier impassive, and so the squadron, great or small, a machine. If the surgeon rates a man as well, he is well. He is loafing if he is not on parade at the call, and must answer for it. If his eye is rolling about and not fixed, if he fumbles inattentively in his drill, or because of the numbness of his hands, if he makes easy times for one foot instead of standing square on both, let him be put in arrest. That

The army discipline.

homesick boy soldier who wept himself asleep on guard, last night, thinking of his mother, was tried this morning and is to be shot after breakfast to-morrow. Pitilessly hard this law of the camp. Perhaps there is no element of justice in it, but if not, there is at bottom a dread military necessity, and by and by the men themselves will discover it. They will have a commander, too, not unlikely, who is much applauded for his fine heroic bearing in some late battle, and will they not begin to be proud of him? Having too a great cause, and doing service with their life for a great country, they will talk their hearts into magnitude by the same, till the tide of sentiment, rising high in their talk, makes their flag a power in the beating of their pulse. So that when the war heat finally is kindled, as it will be soon, nobody thinks any longer of the tough law discipline at which the soldier-life began; for that was meant to kill out all the self-indulgences and private wills, and make clean sweep of all the crotchets and home-bred likings, that could not be taken by the military inspirations. And now when it is done, and the law-force of the beginning appears to be quite gone by, how conspicuous will it be that, in being seemingly forgot, it is being only more grandly fulfilled, than if it were felt in the still unwelcome stress of its intimidations. But nothing any longer goes by the old camp law; for the men will now command themselves, or bid their leader command them, into rougher and more stringent services than the law itself could name. Imagine the forlorn-hope call to be now issued, and that volunteers are waited for; behold every man is ready to go for his company, and all insist on being taken. Why, the christian martyrs, going in before magistrates to confess Christ and die, are scarcely dishonored by comparison with these men who, to keep the commandment of their leader, march out into the jaws of death, and consent to be offered with him for their country. The old precisional drill, that came so hard upon the soldier at first, it will now be seen is even impotent, in comparison with the new army spirit by which it is superseded. Which new force can march the men through rivers up to their waist, and bring them out not knowing they are wet; or can send them to sleep without rations, after a hard day's battle, not knowing they are hungry. They are in the cause; and all such things are the concern of the cause, not theirs. True the old drill is still on hand, but the men know it only as a far-off underground matter that is well enough to be remembered, but no spring of action longer.

We have yet one more example, viz., that which may be cited from the analogies of the civil state. Here we strike an outspreading argument that is wide as the world: for the civil state comprehends all the nations, societies, and ages of humanity. In one view it is a condition based in the necessity of a supreme order, and is, therefore, written down by revelation itself as "the

The civil state.

ordinance of God;" headed by a magistrate in God's name, who is authorized "to bear the sword," and not "bear it in vain." The liabilities of this enforced rule are some of them heavy, such as those for example of military duty and taxation, and the whole scheme of order, considered as maintained by penal sanctions, is naturally unpopular. Yet not as unpopular as we should think, and likely enough to be not unpopular at all. Thus we have always on hand, in these modern times, the question of liberty and law; and a great many have not learned as yet what liberty is. They think it is exemption from law, and that having no law is the true way to be free. Whereas the greatest liberty is where there is most law needing least enforcement; where in fact the penalties are forgot, and well nigh the precept too; so quietly does it sleep back of public memory. Who of us now, but the malefactors and felons wanting to be safe in crime, ever feel a straw's weight of severity in the law, or even think of it as law at all. It is light as air to us, and not less free. We altogether love the shelter of the magistracy, and have it as one of our chief cares to provide a magistracy for ourselves, going into their election with the greatest vehemence of endeavor, as for what we most intensely value. And then our homages will be to them, scarcely at all to the law. We think of them never as dynasties farming their people and the laws for their own benefit. We have not even a jealousy left of that old tyrant magistracy once so oppressive. But we run our recollections back to such great chiefs of statesmanship as William of Holland, and Cromwell, and Washington, and the minor lights closer at hand, who undertake to lead the people for their good. Such magistracy we love and trust, and forgetting the law we only think of liberty.

Now by so many instances, which might be largely increased in number, I have undertaken to show how the grand analogy of letter and spirit, law and liberty, or law and free commandment, runs through all the organific discipline of life and society. Every thing goes on by this double ministration. By these two factors, one preparing the other, and the other partly replacing and completely fulfilling the one, whatever is most perfect and consummately free in character and order, is brought to pass. In this scale of analogies we go up as it were by so many stairs, and make our landing finally, at that last rising where the sinners of mankind pass up out of their low dejection, out of their bondage under law, into liberty and justified life.

I ought, perhaps, to just add, lest we imagine this kind of material to be now exhausted by the specifications made, that exactly the same analogy goes with every law of duty and morality. Every virtue begins at law, and is put lifting there, as a plant underground, till it finally breaks up through, flowering into liberty. Thus it is with temperate living, frugality, simplicity of dress, truth of character, and with all the vices to be kept down—luxury, sensuality, show, covetousness, revenge and jealousy, popularity-loving and ambition, insincerity and hypocrisy. A law goes with every common virtue, and against every corresponding vice, laying on heavy coercions of penal consequence in the first stages of experience, to be no more sensibly felt, after the virtue is set fast, and the spontaneous waft of duty is come. It is only not clear always, in these innumerable varieties of ethical discipline, by what means or modes of transition, the spontaneous condition will be reached. Probably the means will be occasional and various.

Having made this excursion among the analogical sub-gospels of our discipline, let us gather up now some of the helps and coincidences afforded, to assist our argument in the main question. We find then, first of all, a two-factor method, like that of law and grace, employed in almost every sort of training wanted for the advancement of our human state. A beginning is made with law and legal enforcement, and an expectation had of bringing out the subject, by some more inspiring influence added, in a way of spontaneous obedience, which, forgetting the coercion, minds only the principle. A transition is to be made from principle enforced by statute, to principle beheld in its own attractions and accepted in love for its own sake. The good intended in the first stage is perfected in the second as a way of liberty; where the subjects are the more obedient because they are free, and the more free because they are obedient.

But again, the free state, when it is reached, makes no compensation to the law-state, and the law-state makes no demand of satisfaction for the penalties gone by or discontinued. Good sons, and scholars, and workers, and soldiers, and subjects, are at liberty to be good, without any complaint from the law they have broken, or any demand of compensation for the penal sanctions thrown out of right by their becoming so. *No compensation wanted.* The wayward child of his mother, who is grown up into a dutiful manhood, has a long debtor-score stringing back over the lapse of years, but what the reckoning of so much wrong and deserved chastisement may be, neither she nor he can tell. And her law makes no demand of satisfaction; neither has any body so much as a thought of damage to the maternal authority, requiring to be made good. In all these sub-gospel cases, the legal and coercive sanctions go by, as it were, because of their successes; that is because their aims and uses are fulfilled, or come to pass. What better can law do, as a moral institute, any where, than to show itself a basis of freedom in the inspirations of duty. It is represented by the great general, who, having gained the saving of his country, is not gone out of honor and consequence, because he has not still his country to save.

Once more, it is important to observe that, in these analogic cases and examples, the penal enforcements appointed are never destructively meant. They are never punitive, but only coercive and corrective. They have it for their very simple office to give cogency to the law-force, and prepare that assent which makes room for the uncoercive, free-moving agencies, to finish out the duties in their inspirations. The two kinds of action are unlike in the last degree, and yet they are concurrent; one thrusting on from behind by coercive pushes of enforcement, and the other drawing on by the fervid attractions of love and promise. Both together make up the score of so many kinds of discipline, strong in their conjunction, weak or even null in their single operation. Certain evils that we call retributive, such as the woes and horrible exasperations of intemperate drink, do appear, it is true, to be too dreadfully overmastering in their dispossessing force, to be thought of as promotives in any sense of the virtues rejected. And yet we may very well ask, what else but such a cogency of warning can preventively tame the appetite for drink? and what but such a hell in the mind afterward, can ever burn a way out of thrall into sobriety and reason? However nearly destructive any such penal motive may seem, there is, after all, no reason to distrust the beneficence of it. For if any one suggests the possibility of a plan which exposes to no such appetite or danger, that is not God's way; he never lets go a virtue or excuses from it, because it will have to master a great peril, but considers rather that he gives

<small>The penal sanctions never destructive.</small>

us greater opportunity according to the greatness of the peril. And how cheap and slack the poor world's figure would be, going loose in a virtue that does not include the grand, self-keeping masterhood and majesty of continence.

III.

We pass over now to the main subject for which this excursion has been made; viz., God's twofold way of training under his law, and the redemptive grace in his Son. The matter of this training, as we now perceive, is not *The gospel way not peculiar.* so peculiar as to make it a case wholly by itself, but it holds a place, instead, at the head of a vast, widespread system of analogies that, in their lower grade, look up to be its interpreters. It is grounded partly, at least, in the same necessities and reasons, though moving in a scale so transcendent, as to scarcely allow the relationship of its humbler kinsmen to be observed. Here, in this higher discipline, we are asking always What of the law?—in particular, what is to be apprehended for it in redemption? what losses will occur to its authority? what compensations will be needed? what satisfactions must be provided? Where one thing, at least, is quite certain beforehand, which we may have our comfort in, carrying it on with us; viz., that it is the law of God, and is not likely to go down, whatever we may say, or omit to say, or think, or omit to think, concerning it.

That we may have our mark before us, and steady our thought by it, in the inquiries that remain, I now set forth in formal statement the following conclusion, which has been looming up more and more distinctly upon us in all the previous approaches.

General statement.

That our present state of life, or probation, is a state of penally coercive discipline, in which the law, broken by sin, is sufficiently consecrated by Christ, incarnated into and co-operating with it, in his life and cross.

Three points in this proposed summation require to be distinctly stated.

I. The penally coercive discipline. It is not penal, of course, or penalty, in any such sense that it must be destruction, and can not be discipline. In calling it discipline, I call it schooling; for schooling is what we mean by discipline. Calling it our schoolmaster to bring us to Christ, we mean the same thing; viz., that it is promotive, corrective, coercive, no matter what our deserts may be, or what penalties in the principle of desert they would bring us. I use the terms penally coercive discipline, in the understanding that our training toward God is carried on under a motivity thus named, which is not judicially penal, and is not meant to be; for it is not graded by the desert of actions, but by what is wanted for the future benefit and due correction of the actors. I use the term penally coercive, because there is a law sanction in the discipline, coming back upon actions, in a certain

The coercive discipline.

way of retaliation or retributive consequence, without being a substantive measure of their ill-desert; the object being not any making up of award, but the making us aware of what we are doing and becoming. It is the lesson we take in our schooling, to make us understand, stage by stage, ourselves and the law, and to be an efficient element in securing our obedience.

What is penal in our discipline would be penalty, if it were not discipline; nay, it would be justice itself; *i. e.*, justice in its nature, if not in its measure. For it is exactly what the laws of natural consequence inflict in the name of justice; save that here, in this temporal and mortal discipline, they are confronted by a whole array of restraining, mitigating, interspacing powers—Christ, and the Holy Spirit, and the Word, and the Church, and an all-tempering Christly providence—converted in that manner into another sort of economy that, for the present, makes nothing of desert and every thing of benefit, and which, therefore, we call discipline, penally corrective discipline, because it is so far penal as will make it most corrective.

Only it requires to be understood that, in being set for benefit and not for punishment, there is still, at times, an awful severity in it, and the desolations wrought by it, that seem to even smoke with judgment. *Greatness of the discipline.* It clearly enough should be so; for a penally corrective discipline supposes no delicate handling. How shall sin be revealed to itself, save in forbidding and frightful pictures—in diseased bodies, in distempered thought, misadjusted mind, exasperated passion, by incapacities and bondages, anxieties, commotions, terrors of the air and of the ground. Sometimes the picture will almost take on a look of destruction; because only what is close upon destruction has force enough to be decisive. The woes thus of our merely mental experience, sometimes bear an expression of such unpitying severity as compels us even to shudder, in allowing that God is represented in them. Still they are coercive only, and not penal, and it is not for us to say, in any case, that they are more severe than they need be.

By this fearful stress of discipline, without judicial penalty, the due coercive power has been and is to be maintained. The law requires no properly judicial severities for its better enforcement. There is, indeed, a justice penalty, or state of penalty, provided for in God's causations, that is to come into range when the other world opens, but it has been held back here, just to make this a world of probation, as otherwise it could not be. There are here no awards of judgment to be taken out of the way, but the coercive side of the law, and the free grace side of the commandment, work on together, for the same result of benefit; just as in the humbler analogies I have cited from our common life, the law side keeps its footing even after the liberty has come. Who has ever thought it necessary, in the school, to stop at some given point, and take away the coercive rule, to let the free application begin?

If now it be objected that we are already cast, or held in detention, by the bonds of penalty, which must be somehow taken off before we are free to any thing good, that is a mode of speaking which supposes that the law has no function left since the fall but to kill; and that, being once dead, there is nothing left for us but to stay by our death, till another dispensation, working also by itself, appears, to bring us life. But the two are not given to work separately in this manner, but to work together in composing a complex discipline—a coercive law power, to be borne up and consummated by a life-giving personal grace; and a personal-grace power, to be made welcome and efficient by the coercive and appalling arguments of the law. Otherwise, if the two have no joint office, the law has really no benign efficacy at all; it has nothing to do, and never had, but to condemn and kill. We are bound, in just deference to God, to look for something different, and we have no right to be satisfied till we find some righteous moving of benefit in it. As we do, when we find it working even in the cross itself, and composing a discipline with it, for the training and exercise of character. True it is declared to be a killing or slaying power, but we must not hold the figure too literally. As a mere legal discipline, taken by itself, it would do this and this only. It was never meant to be thus taken,

The two factors have no separate working.

but to be a factor of coercion, working with the free-grace factor in Christ, and that in turn a factor with it, both composing the divinely beneficent whole of discipline together. And if any one may insist on seeing what place it has for killing in such a work of benefit, it must be enough to say that, while it commands for good and good only, its command rejected will be found to be unto death—which is only so far death as will make it a more convincing and cogent argument in the discipline. So as long as the disobedience continues, it will be piling greater condemnations, submerging the will under heavier incapacities, increasing the whole inward misrule and disorder, and making the death more dead—a more cogently coercive element, perhaps, for that reason—till finally the subject, appalled by his condition, and visited by some unwonted sense of goodness in the salvation offered him, yields himself tenderly up to that crisis of discipline which makes it the beginning of a better mind and life. And no matter at what period in life, whether early or late, the call to repentance may be made, there is never to be a calling away from the law; for the cogencies of the law are always wanted as truly as the grace of the commandment. They work together, and are of right never to be separated; for the killing factor, so conceived, has a really beneficent office, indispensable to the true result. There are passages, we know, that appear to set the two factors, the killing and the life-giving, completely apart, as when it is said, " For ye are not under the law but under grace." But this is a contrast that holds good only in a certain general way. The meaning can not be that we are not under law as truly as ever, but only that we are not under it as going to be saved in works of legalism by it. The being under grace too, is not a device to separate us from the law—but to beget us anew in the living spirit of it.

II. It is another point to be considered, as regards our supposed scheme of discipline, that while it includes the law of God as a necessary factor in its operation, it must not here be the law as backed by judicial sanctions, but only by such casual, ungraduated sanctions as will duly enforce the discipline. There is accordingly no justice work done here, as we perfectly know. We do not live in a scheme of awards, but in a scheme of probatory discipline. Persons are not treated alike, nor wrongs alike, neither is any thing kept in the scale of desert. God reserves the liberty in his own hands, to turn our experience here in what way of stress or modified comfort will best advance his good purpose in us. At the same time, while nothing is being done with us here in the terms of justice, we are duly notified and certified of a time future, when our present mixed way of discipline will be over, and we shall be carried on with our bad ways uncorrected, if so it must be, to be settled on the hard-pan basis of justice pure and simple, receiving every man according to his work.

Justice after discipline.

Here we touch the province of justice for the first

time, only we have had a certain forelook of it kept alive in us always, which has had great value according to its cogency. And that we may not lose this advantage, ways have been carefully devised to keep the sense of this dread future alive in us, in a perpetually distinct remembrance. For while nothing is ever done here that belongs to justice, our christianity itself undertakes to be a judgment day gospel, and Christ himself to be the judge of the world. There is also going on here always a kind of pre-judicial distribution, which bears a look of justice so impressive, that, by many, it is taken, and even by many preachers preached, as being the very matter of justice itself. It comes in as the retaliatory or *lex talionis* matter of our experience—the same which Christ had in mind when he said, "with what measure ye mete it shall be measured to you again." And so much is there of this retributive style in the facts of the world, that a moderately ingenious person will cite instances enough for a kind of judgment-day show, in vindication of almost any right principle—as if Providence were concerned, by a kind of revolving delivery, to pour the missiles of justice into every offense and offender. And there is beside a certain aspect of validity in these facts of *quasi* retribution. They are such kind of consequences as go with the great coercive law of our discipline, to be its vindicators. We only mistake when we conceive them to be certain or inevitable in their occurrence, and to be graded

[marginal note: Kept apprised of justice to come.]

always in the scale of desert. But irregular as they are and desultory, they make an element in the scene of our discipline that is even indispensable. They show us too that while christianity is engaged to clear us of the dread inexorabilities of justice here, so that we may have our trial in liberty, it still manages to keep us in the clear beholding of them always, that we may not miss the benefit of their cogency.

But what, in this view, of justice as an element of our religious experience—justice in the law, and to be delivered from in the grace of the cross, and justice in the personal character of God? I wish it were not to be expected that some true believers will miss, in the statement I am giving, any such reference to the justice of God as they are wont to indulge, when they magnify the exemption Christ has bought for us by his suffering. I suppose it is partly as a result of this piously meant practice, and partly because the justice of God is closer to the appreciative grasp of their natural understanding, than any other of God's attributes, that they are so prone to be forward in their admiration of it. It comes into their range of thought because it is that attribute of God which uses force, and so becomes the king attribute; as the thunders of Olympus made Jupiter the father of the gods. And yet the word *justice* does not once occur in the New Testament, neither does the word *just* in any single case where it relates to Christ and his death, save in the little expression, " that he might be

<small>What to be said of justice.</small>

just,"* where it should be translated " that he might be righteous." Meantime it is sufficiently clear that God himself does not rate his justice as the fore-front attribute of his nature. He does not say, with sundry teachers who are in the particular type of sensibility that most readily admires this nearly political attribute, justice first, then love and pity afterward. He is willing to have us think of him as slow to anger, but not as slow to righteousness, or love, or patience. And when he is constrained to let some fire-tempest fall on men, he will call it "his work, his strange work, his act, his strange act;"† as if he had short love to it himself. Neither does he ever magnify himself in that he can be evenly just in his judgments—doing always and by all rejectors exactly as they deserve—partly, it may be, because he knows that very imperfect creatures, such as we, can do by our enemies what they deserve, a great deal more easily than we can what is better than they deserve. He will, of course, be upright before all things else, but the dealing back on transgressors what their crimes deserve, is a very different matter. One is God's righteousness, the other his justice; one his act, the other his strange act. Only not so strange that it can not be done when nothing else can be.

And still that such a special and fondly disproportionate esteem should be felt towards the justice of God, when Christ dies to win our deliverance from it, is even the more remarkable, when the reason

---

* Romans iii, 26. † Isaiah xxviii, 21.

stated for his intervention is so palpably bad, so galling morally to our most inborn convictions. If we look into the cases of moral analogy that have been cited—the school, the family, the army—we do not find that we are disturbed lest the law may be losing its penalties because of the obedience and liberty coming in. What were the law and the penalties for, but to be fulfilled in just such obedience and liberty? Or take the case of intemperance and the dreadful woes that are set to be its powers of coercion. Why do not the brothers in humanity who undertake to bring off a victim, feel bound, as vicarious woesmen, to make up the penalties which are going to be taken away, by a contribution of pains that will keep them good. And if they can not give in pains of dissipation, why not give in pains of good behavior? The absurdity of such a proceeding we see without difficulty, but when we come up into the field of religion, we drop out the conception of law as an element of coercive discipline, and take it simply as a thermometric register, to record, for justice, the highest point which the heat of transgression has reached.

And then what has been shown by the said law-register, is going to claim the awards of eternal justice shortly, unless there is a respite obtained by some grace of penal suffering, by which justice is satisfied. *Justice to be maintained by compensation.* The justice of the law, or the justice of God, in other words, is expected to be satisfied by penalties undeserved, contributed by Christ to pay off penalties deserved! And by such a transaction as this it is, that the strangely partial deference to God's justice, of which I just now spoke, is produced by Christ's death. It is an operation which buys God's justice out of the world, where it can no longer be found, and does it by the pains of Christ, which are the pains of innocence! Why, to stay in such a world, where the holiness of God is enveloped in such a nimbus of confusion as to principles, might very well be a hardship. Besides what do we understand by a penalty undeserved? There is plainly no such thing *in rerum natura*. Penalties deserved are simply what a bad deserving may create. But where there is no bad deserving they are out of consequence, and what is more, even out of possible idea. And again, if penalties undeserved are to pay the debt of justice for penalties deserved, the two kinds have no common measure, and how shall we state the equation between them? How much straight line is equal to how much right angle? How much pain of remorse may be duly atoned by how much pain of rheumatism? Shall we change the word then, shall we put the sufferings of Christ against the sufferings of guilty men? Innocent suffering then, to be gotten somewhere, any where, even out of Christ, is to make up the quantum which the law demands for all transgression. Why, such a total, footing up infinite, would even be an offense. Sufferings are too much a drug in God's worlds every where, to allow his making up the honors of his justice in their computation.

But there is still another difficulty by which our theologians of the last century began to be sorely pressed. If the law is satisfied, or the justice of God satisfied, by the contributions of penalty Christ has made in his death, what becomes of justice after that for any body, and where is the possibility left of future punishment for even such as die incorrigible? The common way had been to assert only a partial or particular atonement, made for the elect. But our New England teachers were not quite willing to tell the non-elect that they are down for justice any way, and as little to proclaim a free release to all, on the ground of a general satisfaction. They struck for a new theologic invention, therefore; viz., a public justice for all men, which is no justice in particular, but only a pool for such as may come to repentance, and then a distributive justice waiting for each particular man, who may die in his sins after his day is ended. The public justice is not made by Christ's endurance of any man's penalty, but is a public character of justice made up for God, by what expression of justice may be yielded in Christ's death, conceived to be equal to the expression of justice that would be afforded by all the penalties exacted of all the world. In this view Christ is the virtual substitute or compensation for all the pains of all transgression. Sometimes a different way of statement is adopted, to escape the

Public justice invented.

obvious objection that, as Christ is supposed to suffer what is really nobody's penalty in particular, his suffering can not make any expression of God's justice at all; his death therefore, it is said, expresses the abhorrence of God to sin, as the penalties exacted of all wrong doers would, and so they make up the desired character of justice. How much is gained by this shift of expression will better appear, when it is proved that God's abhorrence to sin can any way find offense in the pure, unsinning beauty of Christ, so as to be expressed by his suffering.

This most sorry theologic invention has had as much credit gained for it as it can bear. It is most distinctly, most provincially new. I know of no scripture that yields it even a complexion of evidence. It discovers two justices, or kinds of justice, one that is for use in this life, and another for the life to come. The meanings are in the last degree artificial, and the modes of their relations to each other, and to sin, and to a possible way of salvation, are too subtle and confused to be distinctly apprehended by any but persons thoroughly practiced in the subtleties. How much better is the very simple, almost self-generated statement I have given—no justice at all in this world; exact, inevitable justice for all incorrigible subjects in the world to come.*

---

* My subject is nowise responsible for what the condition of justice hereafter is to be, but I am so little unwilling to be responsible for what opinions I have in the matter, that I set down a perfectly frank statement of them, and leave it without concern to answer for itself.

III. It now remains to speak of the last and most distinctively christian of the three points named in my general statement, or deduction; viz., that the coercive discipline we are under—including the law element and what elements of Providential enforcement are added—waiting for no pains of justice to re-establish it and re-cement its broken order, is consecrated anew forever, and more than consecrated, endued with transcendent efficacy, by Christ incarnated into it, and dying in it and for it. The coercive

Christ incarnated into the coercive discipline.

---

1. The allotments or awards of justice hereafter will not be made up. it is most agreeable to suppose, by judgment passed on all the particular acts done, but will be the total effect or damage of them, so that every man will suffer just what he is, or has become.

2. The state of future awards will not be a new probation; God would doubtless give us fifty new trials if it would do us any good, but there is not the least probability of any such result, but of great moral damage and confusion rather. (Vid. *One Trial Better than Many,*—Sermons on Living Subjects).

3. Still every bad soul will be forever free, nevertheless, to the beginning of a new life, and will have no doubt of his acceptance in it.

4. The bad society will be separate probably from the good, and that for their own comfort, if for no other reason.

5. From the known effects of wicked feeling and practice in the reprobate characters, we expect that the staple of being and capacity in such will be gradually diminished, and the possibility is thus suggested that, at some remote period, they may be quite wasted away, or extirpated.

6. Of course their suffering will be reduced according to their reduced capacity; for it is no fixed quantity set against the reckoning of old sins, but is always to be grading itself anew, according to what they are and have capacity on hand to be.

discipline was organically framed and set in order for the world, even from the first, and long ages before the appearing of Christ. It included, of course, the law and, beside that, all the vast material of outward expression, such as might second or assist the general endeavor of the discipline—the health or disease of the body, the seasons, the bounties of nature, the oppressions and liberties, the wars, the captivities and migrations, all the private and personal benefits too secret to be named, all the ministries of human love and friendship. These all together are not Christ, but taken as additions to the naked authority of law, they go a certain way to help out its otherwise barely coercive efficacy. But a great and supereminently glorious addition now arrives—Christ is born into the discipline as before in operation, and becomes the quickening life and central factor of it. And this is the change that we celebrate as christianity; a change that is just as great as must needs take place, when the impersonal and dry machine composed of law and world—absolute law and scarcely responsive world—has God's full sensibility and sanctifying life poured in, to moisten the dryness of the discipline and make it a complete gospel. So that now it goes no more by thrustings on of enforcement only, but by such powers of unenforcement as may be looked for, in the suffering love and gentle endurance of the Lamb. The commandment is here come, and the discipline that was like to be too nearly penal, working too much in the way of fear and mere self-interest, and too little in the way of inspiration, is now to be consummated as a way of complete and perfect liberty.

Christ then is here, we now proceed to say, incarnated into the discipline we are under, and membership with us in its adversities and trials; in the enduring of which he is brought into conditions of unspeakable suffering. When we say that Christ is incarnate thus in our humanity, we commonly appear to mean very little by it, more than that he takes on the look and speaks with the voice of a man. We seem to think of him more as a passenger than as a born resident, and we only see him on his way through, doing many beautiful things, and suffering specially nothing except in a sharp theologic crisis at the close. What it means for him to be incarnate, we do not consider deliberately enough to grasp the idea and measure the consequences; and above all the consequences of personal suffering to himself. True it is understood that he is here as one of us for a time, but what special cause of tragedy there may be in that, more than belongs to the average experience of men themselves, we do not perceive. Besides it is the cross, we think, that brought upon him all that was to be accounted specially severe in his experience. His incarnation was no part of his suffering, being only a matter of less cost to him probably than our incarnate state is to us. In this manner we fall out of key as regards any proper estimate of his life; for the par-

His suffering is the incarnation.

ticular crisis of his death, short and sharp as it was, comprised but a very small part of the suffering and sacrifice his mission cost him.

Let us see if we can bring ourselves into a right opinion of what is involved in Christ's incarnation, as respects the matter of his suffering. It means that he is incarnated into common condition with us, under what is called the curse. He could not reach us as a teacher, helper, friend, and Saviour, except by coming into membership with us in our human race itself. No plan to work upon us from a point above us, or one side of us, could operate with any promise of effect. He must become a habitant with us, a fellow nature, a brother, and that he could not be, without being entered into what is our principal distinction as being under the curse. For this does not mean, as many very hastily judge, a state of doom or punition, but simply a condition of discipline ordained for spiritual profit and recovery. It means exactly what I have been setting forth as a condition of coercive discipline, or as I have once or twice called it, a condition of penally coercive discipline—adding that it is penally operative, in no sense of punition or judicial award, but only in a way to impress the consequences and demerit of actions, in such degrees of severity as will best serve the moral benefit of the subjects. The curse, in this view, is all for benefit, only working partly by what is disagreeable or distressful. Underneath was the word of the law, then above are harnessed to it, to work with it, all the multifarious cogencies that make up the total of our life. Christ will suffer nothing as by his own fault, or to correct him in his own wrong, nothing to coerce him in his own choices, and yield him personal benefit in the discipline. He is here for no such purpose, but only to bring himself personally near to us, for our benefit. His incarnation puts him in the compass of all that belongs to the solidarity of the curse, except that he is touched by none of its contaminations. He will suffer of course from the wrongs of wrong-doing men, as truly as if he were one of them himself; and probably as much more severely as the holiness of his life, and the beauty of his actions, will more provoke the hostility of the wicked, and he himself be more tenderly sensitive to injury because of his undefiled sensibility.

Raising now the question, how far Christ must needs come into suffering, by a ministry incarnated into our penally coercive discipline, it may be important for us first to revise, or make up by a new inspection, the inventory of our own suffering. *Scarcely realize our own sufferings.* True as we know it to be, that pains send us into the world, and pains send us out, and that the whole space between our birth and death is thick-set with twinges, and troubles, and bad hours, and real or imagined wrongs, each new successor shuts the gate of oblivion on its preceding out-goer, and we fancy that we really suffer nothing, but are all the while just coasting along the shores of comfort. True we are not so much happy as comfortably not happy, not so much well as without distress. It is much as if an enjoyment were graded for us by a sort of dumb toothache scarcely perceptible. And yet there are times of pungent suffering coming upon almost every one of us—storms of disease, bitter mournings, prospects blasted, treasons in the house—even that large half of the world who think they have been always going comfortably on, have yet suffered immensely in the total of their hurts and fears, and wrongs. There are many, I know, who make it a point of honor to laugh at all such computations of suffering, much as if it were the way of good navigation to throw the logbook overboard and put the foul weather days under oblivion. They had much better keep the log—and use it.

Secondly, we observe that our human suffering does not come by any principle of desert, and therefore make less of it.

<small>No principle of desert in our suffering.</small>

There is plainly enough no law of penalty or justice in it, and that, if we could keep our conscience from sometimes applying it, amounts to something like a discovery, we think, that it has no meaning, and amounts to little or nothing worthy of attention. We do not observe that the main stress of it comes in the principle of solidarity, where, as regards the more deserving, it has even a kind of substitutional look. History is full of it. Suffering is, in a sense, the staple of history. It falls on men by generations, nations, kingdoms, and continents, massing its subjects, and taking them on the side of their social liability and necessity, where the curse of sin falls heaviest. And the woes that pour in thus, by latitudes and longitudes mapped for suffering, are fearful and sometimes horrible even beyond thought—drought, and blight, and frost, and famine, pestilence and plague, earthquake and hurricane, cities on fire, kingdoms soaked in blood—all which come as a good God sends them, partly to show us for our benefit that his discipline overhangs all mortal peoples and affairs; which also, when he wills it, can find how to make itself subduingly felt. It is here, it is everywhere, and it comes in no slight reckoning, as we sometimes sleepily imagine—the whole creation groaneth and travaileth with it.

Thirdly, we fall into another oversight, in turning to no right account the admitted fact that so many of the best, and purest, and sweetest, of the race do actually seem to suffer most. *Why do the best and purest suffer?* It is as if the solidarity-principle just referred to, turned its masses of bad liability down upon these hapless victims of sorrow and distress, to get an argument particular enough for the heavy-going, lumbering world to feel. We think it hard, we ask how can a good God do it? and yet they are the more honored on this account; being chosen for their suffering office, because their suffering will draw sympathy, and thaw out the frozen apathy of such as, deserving to suffer themselves, could suffer only with small effect. Who will care what they may suffer themselves? what human tear will they set flowing, when they only take their pains in due proportion? But there is a feeling loosened always by the terrible woe that a good man suffers after the Christly fashion, by which we are all the more tenderly affected, that he appears to be suffering, not on his own account as truly as on ours. Most beautiful is the office which these lower, sub-Saviour sufferers are called to fill. And how touching is the argument they give us, to correct the mistake into which we so commonly fall, when we recollect that Christ is the exceptional man, upon whom no penalty can fall, and let ourselves down thus upon the impression that his liabilities of suffering are smaller even than if he were a strictly human person. It does not occur to us that in being pure and spotless far beyond the examples just referred to, he may be chosen of God to go as far beyond them in suffering, as they beyond their fellows.

Just here, saying no more of our under-estimate of Christ's suffering, in the under-estimate we have of our own, I think we may begin to feel the window lifted Suffers greatly because of his purity. where the fresh air blows, and to have the suffering of Christ's mission opened to our discovery, in a way to cause no revulsion. He suffers heavily because he is pure, and just according to his purity; for there is nothing in him to sort with the curse he is under. The blight, the pain, the stormy troubles, and the bitter hate are not for him. His pure, sweet nature, tainted by no evil touch or stain, the immense sensibilities of his divine innocence, recoil from the gentlest penalties, with a feeling dreadfully revolted, such as we, in the blunted sensibility of sin, can not even imagine. It is as if the condemnations of God were upon him —as they are on all the solidarities of the race into which he is come. The disgusts generated in the penal discipline of character, fill his pure, great feeling with revulsions known to him, but unimaginable by us. He suffers all the suffering of mankind, not as we do in mere sympathy with the suffering itself, but as beholding it in its guilty causes—loathing it because it is so base, because of its fallen glory, and because it is so bitterly poisoned by injustice to God— a suffering in which the displeasures of God and his compassions are united by a conjunction that is itself the utmost possibility of suffering.

It is also another aggravation of Christ's suffering, that he has so much mind, and a perception so piercing, to apprehend the utmost significances of acts, and causes, and consequences. *Suffers according to his amount of mind.* Little minds have little sufferings, according to the insect measures of their possibility. What do we better know than that minds in high culture are capable of greater pains under insult and wrong? Thus if such a man as Wordsworth, or Goethe, or Pascal, or Cavour, had been taken captive by some wild cannibal race, and compelled to look on the preparations for his sacrifice, it would not be so much the dread of death that would cost him suffering, but it would be the horrible conception of being himself incorporate in these ferocious and disgusting monsters. His tastes, his imaginations, his conception of what belongs to all dear sensibility in life, would set him in convulsive shudder. In which we have only a most feeble, far-off illustration of what the great Christ-soul must suffer in the approaching scenes of the crucifixion. He had come down out of the upper world, where he had been partaker, from the first, in all God's opinions and sentiments concerning sin. He did not conceive that the crowds of raging persecutors gathered about him were simply unfortunate or lunatic, but that they were maddened penally by their discipline, for though it was not on them as in punishment, it was powerful enough in its wild exasperations, to show them what sin is, and raise a frightful argument against it. He saw their curse in their sin, and the pungency of his suffering was according to the full and divinely cultured perception he had of it, of its relations to God and the world, and of the possibilities of character. He had read the true conception of it in the bosom of the Father, and now he has it on him and feels the horrible touch of it. These bloodthirsty Fijis of the priesthood and the people are conspiring his death. What a conception, that a being so great, so interlocked with divinity, is going here to be actually murdered! does he not, should he not, feel it himself, according to the perception he has of its criminality and the astounding impressions it will raise in all the good great minds of the glorified. What a response has he in it to the all-sacrificing and most tender love in which, by his act of incarnation, he takes the sin of the world upon him and makes his life a sorrow.

Once more, Christ suffers the more heavily, no doubt, that he is in a failing cause. And the misery is not so much that it appears to fail, as that it should be thrown and trampled by just that which only the penal madness of the world could incite. *Suffers in a failing cause.* It sinks under the hatred of goodness, such hatred as only bigotry instigates, by the arts and semblances of hypocrisy. And this hatred hovers about his path in all his rounds of ministry, dogs him in his journeys, makes a larger and continually widening conspiracy. By and by his disciples begin to act shyly, and apparently try to get away from him. Only the dear children, as it were to show how much more reliable inspiration is than prudence, cling to him still, and pay him their heaven-lifted Hosannas, when the full-grown wise drop away. He is therefore in a double sorrow now, that his disciples, who so much need his presence to keep them in any sort of courage as respects the faith of a kingdom, are going here to encounter a loss they are little qualified to bear, and he himself to encounter a far greater loss from their desertion, in the stress of his last hours. O what a hell of selfishness and falsity is this, that such a friend as Christ can not fasten the faith of his friends! It even puts a lot of shame upon him, that he has undertaken to do and suffer so much for creatures so bereft of dignity by the awful undoing of their sin. Could he look on heroes gathering to him and round him, ready to bear his cross after him, souls made great and strong by his presence among them, it would greatly mitigate the pain of his approaching fall. But to see all courage oozing out, and all faith vanishing, in advance of his fatal hour, adds a touch of ignominy to his end more nearly insupportable than any other.

Let us glance now at three or four of the scenes where Christ's great suffering is most remarkably displayed, and also the fact that he has it upon him, consciously, as the curse or penal shame and disaster of our transgression. First, I name the temptation, at which his public life began. Incarnated into the curse of the world, he is now to have his part in a state demonized by evil; and it will be the point of his first great trial to master all the physical taint of his birth, and so far humanly corrupted participation. Another storm, let loose upon him by the new-born consciousness of his Messiahship is the felt solidarity of the sin-wrath, rolled in now so tempestuously, that it takes a whole forty days to get that full possession of himself and his plans, that will enable him to go out upon his work. Meantime he is closeted in the grim wilderness, wrestling with the troubles that crowd upon his mind and disturb his counsel, and even forgetting that he is hungry. Angels come about to minister, and

The temptation.

it appears to be intimated that the wild beasts are drawn together round him, by strange sympathy with some awful sorrow perceptible even to them. It is not common to class this scene with other scenes of suffering in Christ's life, but it has an aspect dreadfully forlorn, and a sin-stamp quite unmatched unless by the crucifixion.

The weeping of Christ over the city is told in fewer words, but it is the more important because it is so casual in the occurrence as to show what feeling he is in habitually—what mountain loads of sorrow from the blasted, guilt-stricken world are always upon him—"If thou hadst known in this thy day the things that belong to thy peace, but now they are hid from thine eyes!" *His weeping over the city.*

But we pass, at this point, to the agonies so called of the garden and the cross, both of which are often conceived to borrow their intensity of suffering from the wrath or justice of God, let fall upon the sufferer that he may take the brunt of our penalty, and compensate or satisfy the law in our behalf. "The cup," it is imagined, can mean nothing less than this. It can not be the "cup of *trembling*," or "the cup of *astonishment*," but must be "the cup of justice," because nothing less than the justice-power of God's hand upon the sufferer, could produce such demonstrations. *The cup and the agony.* It may be so, but I see not how any one can be sure that he might not suffer as severely under the solidarity principle or the world's penal-sanction causes, as he would under justice. Be that as it may, we have a most improbable, perfectly incredible mixture, when he is set before us, under such a conception, calling on his poor disciples, in his awful prostrations, to stay by him and help him—yes, help him to bear God's justice! To his groaning on the ground, and his body dripping blood from the pores, they might possibly give the comfort of a little sympathy, but if he is being wrenched in this manner by the justice of God, what right have they to help him against that? True the suffering is strangely severe, and yet indications of the same kind are reported as having sometimes been observed in the case of men suffering under great mental distress. Morever demonstrations of this nature appear to be quite sufficiently accounted for, when three facts are brought together; (1,) the structural frailty of the physically human person, too little able to support the reactions of a superhuman sensibility; (2,) the extraordinary movement on that sensibility, by the madness and wild exasperation of so great multitudes hasting to precipitate themselves unwittingly on him in a deed that comprehends both sacrilege and murder; (3,) the mortal exhaustion that has now come upon him by his brotherhood relation, so long continued, with humanity; where he has nothing to receive, only wrongs and disgusts to bear, and sympathy and suffering patience to give.

As regards the cross, taken often for a scene of divine justice, the argument would be much easier and better supported, if the problem were to show that the justice displayed is a visitation of God upon the people. They really seem to do all in a way of judicial blindness, and take on the lunatic airs of their dispossession, in ways of cunning and prejudice and passion that completely represent the penal madness of sin—Pilate, Herod, Caiaphas, the soldiers, the multitude, all in character under the curse together. And when that awful word is spoken—"This is your hour, the power of darkness," we even shudder at the suggestion. And yet it is not these, we hear, but Christ himself who is under the ban of justice! Innocence gibbeted and dying by what every body pronounces the most horrible murder on record, he is having laid upon him, we are told, the justice of God, and these monsters in their murder are God's ministers, doing the justice upon him! The mixture of idea, character, and fact—the Good Being using wickedness, and wickedness doing the honors of justice—make up a compound so incongruously bad that we are cruelly revolted by it. Yes, but the Saviour cries out himself—"My God, my God, why hast thou forsaken me?" And this, we are taught, is a plain declaration of the judicial withdrawment of the Father. Does any human creature then believe that Christ is actually complaining here, in his last breath, of being left to die deserted of God, or under the ban of his justice? Interjections are never to be taken pathologically in this manner; for what is this outcry but an interjection of distress vented in scripture words crowding at the

No law of justice over the crucifixion.

moment on his brain? And he as little means that
God has deserted him as the Psalmist himself who
was coming out shortly in praise—" For he hath not
despised nor abhorred the affliction of the afflicted,
neither hath he hid his face from him, but when he
cried unto him he heard."* God had forsaken him,
yet now he finds that he had not hid his face! Furthermore what does Christ promise the poor malefactor dying at his side, but that he shall be with him
this very day in paradise? He seems to have forgotten that he is under the justice of God! Was he not
also saying a little while ago in glorious confidence—
" Therefore doth my Father love me because I lay
down my life for the sheep." And again—" I have
glorified thee on the earth, and now I come to thee."
And again, about the same time, in the same confidence—" Thinkest thou that I can not now pray to
my Father, and he shall presently give me more than
twelve legions of angels?" It could not on the whole
be more clear that Christ came to his cross in the full
consciousness of the Father's loving accord and
sympathy, and that on the cross itself, he was hover-
ing in thought round the gates of paradise just waiting to be opened, and beholding, close at hand, " the
glory that he had with the Father before the world
was."

IV.

I intimated some pages back a design to examine a
few of the principal texts most commonly and con-

---

* Psalms xxii, 1 and 24.

fidently cited, to show that Christ was dealing with God's justice in the suffering of the cross, and that, in this great transaction with justice, we are to conceive him as fulfilling the principal errand of his ministry. Many persons will be held by a certain traditional ring of scripture in such authorities, and will not think it possible that these passages, so deeply imprinted by the iteration of years, have been really turned away from their original meaning by clumsy and false uses, and made to give a testimony that was never in them.

I wish it were possible in advance to rid ourselves of a certain hard-favored, narrow literalism, that lives on proof-texts made by paying no regard to the poetic genius of religious language, and by seizing on single clauses that, in figure, seem to favor a certain point, paying no regard to other clauses in other figures, that require to be accepted as qualifiers and correctives. This whole proof-text region has a most sterile, truth-forsaken aspect, and no ploughing through it of ridicule and remonstrance, appears to do much for it. The man who pours in a pitcher of milk to raise a cream on the sea, has about the same chance of success.

We have no literal language for religious ideas. The exactest things that can be said must be somehow taken as in figure, as when Christ made answer to Peter —that one must forgive his brother not seven times only, but " until seventy times seven." There

No literal language for religion.

we have it, as by arithmetic, but the man who should go back on his multiplication table, and draw out his conclusion that we are to forgive just four hundred and ninety times, would even raise a smile among the proof-text scholars; and none the less, if he were to add, that the number seven is a sacred number, to be exactly taken always, according to the proper exactness of reverence! In the expression of religious ideas we are ourselves under the same law. Thus I knew a little child who had been kept back some time from the story of Christ's death, lest she might be overmuch shocked by it. She was abundantly shocked when it was at length given her, as her evening prayer made evident—"O Lord I am sorry you died; I wish you had not saved us!" "The wicked little reprobate," some fiery St. Dominic of the former ages might have exclaimed, but our literal teachers now would, I think, be a little more lenient. Was there ever, in fact, a more genuinely touching, sweeter prayer? Though taken by the letter, it would not be as good.

But there is a more particular consideration here that has a more particular application; viz., that terms of praise and personal gratitude almost always carry an over-tinted color, and set their subject forth in some <small>Gratitude is free to exaggeration.</small> picturesque way of success. In an old Roman prison more or less infected with poison from the region of malaria not far off, destructive fevers come and go, and many of the prisoners die. At length word is brought to a certain monk of the city, who has learned to follow his Master well and faithfully, that a notable prisoner, long time ago his private enemy, is beginning to show the tokens of the fever. Whereupon the godly monk says—" I must go to him then, since he is my enemy, trying, if I can for Christ's sake, to save him." He goes. By his faithful nursing and attendance the criminal is recovered, and he himself, taking the infection, dies. Now in turn the rescued man, throwing out his soul in words, vainly tries to express the inexpressible tenderness of his obligation. He writes and talks nothing but gratitude all his life long—testifying " O he bore my punishment "—" he became the criminal for me "—" stood in my lot of guilt "—" suffered all the bitterness of my bad desert." It will not be strange if he goes a long way beyond the redemptive fervors of Scripture to say—" he took my debt of justice "—" satisfied the judgment of the law "—" bore the very sins I put upon him "—meaning, of course, nothing more than what he had been saying before. Finally, some time after the parties are gone, when their story itself is fading away, some one undertakes to make up his account of it; and, dull-headed, blind-hearted literalist that he is, he takes up all the fervors of expression just recited, showing most conclusively from the words, that the good monk actually got the other's crime imputed to him, took the guilt of it, suffered the punishment, died in his place, and satisfied the justice of the law that he might be released. The application of this belongs to almost all the scripture terms we have in question.

The strongest and most relied on probably of all the proofs of a judicial significance in the case is this— Christ made a curse for us. "Christ hath redeemed us from the curse of the law, being made a curse for us; for it is written, Cursed is every one that hangeth on a tree."* But observe here, at the outset, that the curse of the law is exactly not the justice of God, but the penal-sanction discipline we are under. For the reference here is not to the denouncement by Moses of outward damage and loss, arrayed as curses to deter the people from disobedience,† —for Christ certainly had not undertaken a redemption from these —but to what is called more distinctively the curse at the original institution of our penal discipline itself.‡ Into this, as we have seen, Christ was incarnated, and here was to be the field of his redeeming work. It only occurs to the apostle as a verbal coincidence, though a little out of line as to any precise accord of meaning, that Christ crucified is to be more fitly called a curse, that any malefactor left hanging on a tree is by a maxim of the law so regarded—"Cursed is every one that hangeth on a tree."§ The rhetoric of his gratitude scorns detention by an over-nice verbal exactness. Enough that he will magnify Christ's coming down to be with us, under the world-blight of our sin, where the corporate frenzy, rage and hate trample and tear his divine person as if he

---
* Gal. iii, 13.   † Deut. xxviii, 16–19.   ‡ Gen. iii, 14–19.   § Deut. xxi, 23.

were no better than a malefactor, as he is a member now of the race. The retributive liability he is in, is severe enough to bear even a look of justice. We only happen to know that no suffering of our own under the curse is justice, and that he is suffering with us in our lot as it is. If we call it penal, as I have called the disciplinary sanctions arranged for us, it is not the penality of justice.

Peter declares himself in terms very different as to figure, but closely correspondent in idea, "Who his own self bare our sins in his own body on the tree, that we, being dead to sin, should live unto righteousness; by whose stripes ye were healed."* It is difficult here to imagine that he himself very closely considered the items, or sub-clauses of his statement—how the sins came into Christ's body without making him a sinner, and how, not being a sinner, he bore them, and what for, and with what effect—but two things are specially evident in his words, and in these their main significance lies; (1,) that Christ is so far entered by his incarnate personality, into the curse, or penal woes of transgression, that he has them in himself, and is lifting them off by the beautifully softened power he gives them in the felt conjunction of his suffering sympathy; (2,) that no thought of compensation is here being made to God's justice, for the terminal effect is to be in us; "that we being dead to sin should live unto righteousness." Besides it is to have its effect like all penal-

The declaration of Peter.

---
* 1 Peter ii, 24.

sanction discipline, in a complete healing up of all the scars of transgression—" By whose stripes ye were healed." In the next chapter Peter holds the same general idea—" For Christ also hath once suffered for sins, the just for the unjust, that he might bring us to God."* It is not said that he suffered in the terms of justice to buy us off from justice, but simply in self-sacrifice to bring us off.

Sometimes Christ's own language is cited, when he declares that " the Son of Man came, not to be ministered unto, but to minister, and to give his life a ransom for many."† Is not a ransom a price paid commonly to buy off captives and criminals? Yes, and very commonly not. " I will ransom them from the power of the grave,"‡ does not mean that God will make payment to the grave for obtaining a release. To hang the conclusion of a judicial satisfaction for sin upon this mere word, just as capable of an idea less revolting, is a very sad illustration of what the proof-text making process may do. How different the dear great thought of Christ when he says, I came to minister and not to buy, to offer up my life as the quickening power of unbought life in you. And this word bought, " bought with a price," we need not go over the same argument concerning that.

Christ gives a ransom.

It was most natural that the putting over of sins upon criminals, and especially on the head of the goat, to signify by his being

The scape-goat.

---

* 1 Peter iii, 18.   † Mark x, 45.   ‡ Hosea xiii, 14.

driven out into the wilderness, the deportation of sin, should become a favorite symbol often of the beautiful office taken by Christ, in the assumption of our sadly broken, dreadfully enthralled state. As when Paul declares, "For he hath made him to be sin for us, who knew no sin; that we might be made the righteousness of God in him."* I will not go into any argument here to show that no sin of ours ever could be entered into the pure soul of Christ, or could stay there for one mortal breath without being burned up in the flame of his purity. The apostle plainly enough means to assert no such assumption or transference, but simply that Christ bowed himself on our lot of sorrow and painful, wrathful disorder, in a mind to die into us and let us die with him. Becoming sin for us in this manner, his hope is that we may be made the righteousness of God in him. Not that imputed righteousness which many think evens up the score of justice, but that living righteousness, also in a different sense imputed, which is the righteousness of God himself, and is "by faith unto all and upon all them that believe."

It now remains to take a little more deliberate review of the fifty-third of Isaiah, which, I think, may well be rated as the most wonderful of all human compositions. We have in it a general stock fund opened of vicarious images and offices, set forth as pertaining to a certain nameless person never heard of, and visibly quite unknown to the Isaiah's meaning stated.

---

* 2 Cor. v, 21.

prophet himself. Far back in the dark of his only half-historic time, when the Greeks are scarcely beginning to be Greece, he brings forth his man of the cross, showing him only by tokens that he does not understand himself; and the picture is so Christly, that criticism, turning every way and searching right and left for some original in story, or poetry, out of which it could be made, is obliged to utterly fail and desist. If heaven was ever opened, it was opened here, and the note of vicarious function, running like a voice of litany through so many terms and images, softens our wonder into worship. All the greater reason that we should not let our reverence be turned to superstition by the narrow, over-stringent literalism of our interpretation. Thus when the Evangelist Matthew* says of Christ and his healings, "That it might be fulfilled which was spoken by the prophet Esaias, Himself took our infirmities and bare our sicknesses," a very little good sense will forbid our imagining that Christ literally took all the diseases of his patients—their fevers, blindnesses, palsies, leprosies—on himself; and will put us under a caution against the too literal construction of the other figures which follow.† When the prophet says, "wounded for our transgressions, bruised for our iniquities," it is not to be doubted that he conceives some kind of penal infliction in the suffering endured. And then the question follows, whether it is the penalty of our state of discipline, or of justice itself, which

---
* Matth. viii, 17. † Vid. Note p. 41–5, former treatise.

has no place in this present world? And then still another question, whether the two prepositions *for* mean *for* as in payment for our transgressions, or only *for* in the sense of being incurred by him in his engagement in our behalf. It is important also to note the final clause—" and with his stripes we are healed," where the figure of healing gives a function to the suffering that never can be made to go with justice— justice does not heal. It follows " and the Lord hath laid on him the iniquity of us all," and perhaps we take it as a solemn announcement of the very impossible fact that our sins are literally transferred to the sufferer. Whereas it is plainly enough, as we just now saw in another example, a form of language generated by the scapegoat ceremony, where the priest confesses the sin of the people on the head of the goat, and he is driven off into the wilderness to signify the deportation of the sin. The sin is not on the goat, the whole ceremony is vehicle, contrived to signify, as in form, simply God's deliverance of the people from their guilt. So when the Lord lays the iniquity of us all on the divine sufferer, deportation, deliverance, not punition, is the gist of the meaning. Another phase of the picture is brought forward, when the prophet says—" Yet it pleased the Lord to bruise him, he hath put him to grief." The Jewish habit was to refer every thing good and bad to God's will—" Is there evil in the city and the Lord hath not done it?"—and precisely how far the prophet would go in ascribing the " bruising " and the " grief " to

God's will, in distinction from the wrong doing of wicked men, we may not be able to say, but if, in some sense, he would charge it all to God's infliction, it does not follow that the infliction is judicial penalty; for it can as well be penal-sanction suffering, as we certainly know that all other suffering in this world is. In the same verse again the prophet calls up a sacrificial image—"When thou shalt make his soul an offering for sin." But an offering for sin takes it away, never as being payment for it, but as being a token that expresses contrition; in that way a liturgical help to repentance—just that which Christ is to be, in a much higher and more competent way, in the sacrifice of his death. Once more we read—"he bare the sin of many, and made intercession for the transgressors." This word bare is not a word of punishment, but a word of burden; signifying the charge or load which a friend takes on him, in the woe or fall of another, by the stress of his own vicarious concern for him. Thus God was declared to be afflicted, in the affliction of his people, and to bear and carry them all the days of old. Thus also Paul exhorts the Galatians—"Bear ye one another's burdens, and so fulfill the law of Christ;" meaning by the law of Christ the life, the manner, the spirit of Christ—in a word, the commandment. We come out thus, at the close of this wonderful chapter, chanting its liturgy of sorrow and vicarious passion, long ages before the Suffering Unknown Man appears; having seen how the wrong, the curse, the penal blight, the general sin-stamp marks every thing in the picture, and how he, with it and not of it, ministers by suffering and blood to make intercession for the transgressors; and yet we have come upon no token here of a judicial substitution, or a judicial suffering, or of any thing done for the satisfaction of justice in the payment of its penalties.

It only remains now to sum up the results arrived at, as regards the subject matter of the chapter. The law part of our coercive discipline was never expected to establish obedience and righteousness by itself; neither was it expected to be a complete government by itself, letting no other means or method intervene to bring away from its condemnations, without first paying up its dues of penalty. On the contrary it was designed, from the first, to be joined with other means, working by other methods, and both together to make up the complete order of discipline for men; which discipline is to be kept on foot with every man even to the last, no part of it being displaced by substitutional or compensatory agencies. One part never brings away from the other, and has of course no price to pay for release by the other, the common concern of both being how to fashion a character of perfect obedience and righteous liberty. At first the law and its enforcing agency has greater prominence in the discipline, and appears to be less conspicuously helped by the attractive and gracious powers that are to operate conjunctively with

Results of the argument.

it. These are the good inspirations of public history, the great acts and characters of righteous men, the bounties and beautiful things of the world, the blessings of health and family and property, great escapes and deliverances from peril, the festivals and rites of religion, the hymns of the temple worship and the word of the prophets, all working with the law as gracious and softening influences, to raise up fear into love, and obedience into liberty. These and such as these were the powers that went before, to represent Christ in the discipline, down to the time of his full appearing; and then from that time on, the discipline begins to seem rooted almost wholly in him and his glorious overshadowing personality. The legal aspect is now no longer prominent, and the law appears to be fulfilling itself in the commandment. The discipline we called coercive, takes on the look of a saving power, and we call it a gospel of salvation. We find a full competence in it now to the mastery of sin. The motivities of the law, acting always by appeals to self-regard, operate strongly by the vice of their very nature, to fasten the bad state of sin, and make it a state of thrall. That death-fall, that collapse of possibility, by which man is so fatally broken, as regards any gathering up of himself into good, is even made more hopeless, or at least scarcely more hopeful, by the pressure of mere legal enforcement, for the fault of it is that the motivities and the man are on the death-side of sin together. It can press the subject on, but it can not draw him off. What is wanted here is a new motivity, inspirational in its nature, spontaneous, and free. And therefore it is that Christ comes over into our discipline from his own divine side, and brings his everlasting liberties with him. So that being incarnated into and dying into our world-discipline with us, his glorious and sublime personality overtops every thing in it and us beside. He can show us, and does, how liberty can even die, and he gives it as our tender call of brotherhood to die with him, into his liberty. For now, and by our faith in his person or transcendent personality, we both die and live, and the mastery of our sin is complete. The abstract, tabulated law is fulfilled and crowned in the personal commandment.

Equally true it would be, at the same time, if we should invert all this, and say that the law itself is made personal by the insertion of the Christly love and feeling into it. We are wont to imagine, and are all the while saying, that it is the sin of sin to be taking down the authority of law; and we sometimes think of it as a hard, non-elastic and frangible pillar, flawed and broken, which can no way be repaired, and can only be replaced on payment, by something different; whereas all the grand authority it had, and more, is made good by the tonic life and sovereign vigor of the cross. It is as if the tables of the ten commandments themselves, after Moses threw them down, were mended by passover blood sprinkled on them. So when Christ dies into the law, it becomes itself commandment written out in blood and sacrifice; as much more sovereign over human hearts and consciences as it is more thoroughly personal, and having an authority from the cross which no thunder of Sinai could impress.

It is not our conclusion then, that the commandment takes away from the law, or the law from the commandment, but that they mutually endow and uphold each other; locked together in a complete whole that is one and indivisible. God, we say, never made any so great misfit in a plan as to organize a great first half of it, that he must somehow, any how, at any cost, get rid of, before he could bring it on to success. That is not his way. On the contrary his beginning will reach through to his end, and the law and law-sanctions, never abated or bought off, will be working faithfully on, with all the gracious powers and tender motivities in Christ—part and parcel with them, in the one comprehensive purpose; even as the lightnings and the dews take part together in the growth of the world.

CHAPTER III.

JUSTIFICATION BY FAITH.

We most properly begin our discussion of this great subject at the text of Scripture whence, in a sense, it has its own beginning—" Whom God hath set forth to be a propitiation, through faith in his blood, to declare his righteousness, for the remission of sins that are past, through the forbearance of God; to declare, I say, at this time his righteousness, that he might be just, and the justifier of him which believeth in Jesus."*

The first clause of the passage respecting propitiation has been expounded already in the chapter given on that subject. Our present concern is with the latter clause, relating to the alleged declaring of God's righteousness and the purpose or intent of it.

The " declaring " here intended is not so much a declaring in words, but more in a way of manifestation; as by the facts and acts of Christ's incarnate ministry, considered as the revelation made of his divinely great character, which is itself the righteousness of God. The original word for the declaring is *in-showing*, *endeixis*, that which, being displayed inwardly, begets an inward impres-

<small>Rom. iii, 25–6, how understood.</small>

---

* Rom. iii, 25–6.

sion. It is more important, however, rightly to conceive what the declaring, or in-showing, is for; viz., that when God's excellence is declared, it will both show us how, and why, he was able to overlook, or pass by, the sins of past ages which he suffered in so great forbearance;* and how, as respects the sins of this present time, he is able to be "just" enough, that is great enough, in the power of his "righteousness" to make righteous him that believeth—every one, that is, whose heart is opened by faith to the possible reception of his character. For this, if we rightly understand our word, is what justification signifies. It is that which takes away our condemnation; setting us in confidence with God, by setting God in upon us, in such transforming power that we become new-charactered from his righteousness.

If now it should seem that I put a strain of hard practice on these words "just" and "justify," when Our confusion of words. I convert them in this manner to "righteous" and "make righteous," it must be enough to answer, that the hard strain came long time ago, when the "righteous" and "make righteous" were displaced by "just and justify," and torn away from their natural kinsman "righteousness," in the beginning of the sentence. By a most singular fatality it has come to pass, in this manner, in our English version, that where the Greek Testament gives us three words, noun, adjective, and verb, *dikaiosunē, dikaios,* and *dikaiounta*—all of one root,

---

* Vid. Tholuck in loco.

we have two sets of words in the English to represent them; one from the Saxon, *righteousness*, and two from the Latin, *just* and *justify*. Whence it results that as the Latin words *justitia*, *justus*, &c., have two sets of meanings; a legal or judicial, as pertaining to the penal redress of crimes, and a moral, as relating wholly to character; the two nationalities of tongue in our English version throw us into a jumble of ambiguities, where we have as good chance of mental confusion as the worst enemy of truth could desire.

I really wish it were possible to be rid of these Latin-born terms; for that syllable *jus* puts us thinking inevitably of something done for law and justice, and gravitating always downward on ideas simply political; when we perfectly know, or may, that the Greek words translated by them have never any but some far-off reference to law and justice, even when applied to men, and much less can be expected to have when used as staple words, to signify the moral excellence, or holiness, or righteousness of God, set forth to quicken righteousness in us, and beget in us a character graciously derivative from his. Plainly enough there is no such quickening, reproductive power in justice.

This very strange anomaly of our English version even challenges attention from the scholars now engaged in a version of our scriptures. There probably is not another version in the world that does not translate these three words all by words of the same stock, and it is a verbal wrong and corruption of learning not to do it. Thus even Luther, whose theology, at this point, bore a stamp of legalism so decisive, translates nevertheless—"declare the righteousness," "that he may be righteous," and "make righteous"—*gerechtigkeit, gerecht sei,* and *gerecht mache*-. The Douay and other French versions, following naturally the Vulgate, read *justice, just* and *justify.* And it is also a fair question whether it would not be better for us to get all our three words from the Latin instead of retaining our present very absurd mixture. For it will be seen that the expression "to declare the justice of God" would then have to be expounded so as to carry only the moral idea of righteousness; when of course the other two words would naturally follow the lead which the first has given.

It is, in fact, the sense of our Scripture that all these words are to have a moral, never a forensic, or judicial, significance. For in the Old Testament the noun is translated righteousness, times without number, and when translated justice, as it is twenty-five times, it is justice always in the sense of righteousness. The adjective is also translated righteous on almost every page, and just, always in the moral sense, about fifty times. There may sometimes be a semblance of judicial meaning in the translations of the verb, but the semblance even is commonly doubtful. The Hebrew has a causative mood for the verb, called the Hiphil, and our principal question here relates to the meaning under that mood, as in the word *justify*—*i. e.,* just-make, or cause to be just, or pass as being just. Is it this judicially, or morally, as if it were to righteous-make, or cause to be righteous? "Turn many to righteousness," is the translation of Daniel's causative;* "justify many," the translation of Isaiah's†—where the words translated are exactly the same. Plainly enough there is no thought here of the many being judicially acquitted, but in both cases only of their being made, or caused to be righteous. In the New Testament the noun is always translated righteousness, never justice; the adjective, righteous about fifty times, and just, about thirty, though never in the judicial sense, unless it be in the text we have under examination; the verb is always translated to justify, because we have no other causative or Hiphil word in English, to fill the place. But who can imagine that these two latter words *just* and *justifier* are intended to be taken away from their family relation with righteousness in the very same sentence, and made to carry a different and more legal meaning? There was never such an example of bad writing in the world.

Perhaps it is too much to expect that the three words here in question will ever be substituted by three words in the same root-rela- No relief, truth tion. In that case what appears to must consent to be the unquestionable truth of our in- her disadvantage. terpretation must consent to hold a place of disadvantage and maintain itself, unsteadied by the scripture help it would have from a more homogeneous

---

* Daniel xii, 3.   † Isaiah liii, 11.

translation. Probably, however, no very great detriment would be suffered if due care were always taken to understand the words *just* and *justify*, as having, like the word *righteousness* that precedes, a purely moral significance—that God is just as being righteous, and justifies simply as communicating his own character, and becoming thus a righteousness upon us. Hitherto this caution has not been observed by theologians, and the words have been very commonly construed by them under the judicial analogies. Indeed, the very clause, thus commonly abused, is continually cited as authority to show that it ought to be! Does it not read "that he might be just?"—just, that is, and yet the justifier, because he has so exactly satisfied the immutable justice by his sufferings! How can a text of scripture keep its balance when it is already overset by the bad theology it has created under its bad interpretation, wanting still the bad interpretation to keep itself alive? The prospect in this view, that any concurrent interpretation will somehow be reached, is at least remote. As Protestants we very generally agree that there is a gospel truth which is fitly to be called justification by faith. We acknowledge it even commonly, to be the *articulus stantis vel cadentis ecclesiæ;* but as yet we have only a semblance of agreement in it. Some deny it altogether as they think, who yet more practically believe in it than others who maintain it. We do not agree as to what the justification means, and we differ as much as to what is the meaning of the faith. Great multitudes accept the doctrine only to fight for it as an idol of sectarian opinion. A wiser and more truly christian multitude find their heart's rest in it, and are in it as the peace and liberty of God. Of these latter, too, many who have learned to believe more academically and scholastically than is convenient, give it still a form in their doctrine, which is not the truth discovered in their hearts, and make a church article of it, as Luther himself did, which is only impossible and revolting.

Now this remarkable want of agreement is largely due, as I conceive, to the impossible problem almost always on hand; viz., to make out a rational statement of what in fact does not exist, a justification that stands in the satisfaction of God's law and justice. I propose, accordingly, to open the discussion at this point; removing if possible the false assumption referred to. The law, it is conceived, must be satisfied, or the penalties must be satisfied, else there is no possibility of deliverance; for God will be false to his law and justice, if he does not somehow provide what makes the release of transgression consistent with the honors of his government. Christ therefore has contributed in penal suffering, we are told, what exactly compensates the law, or evens the score of justice; so that he who believes may be justified —legally justified. Or according to another scheme which is different, and is called the governmental scheme, God's justice will consist in the expression made by his penalties of his hatred or abhorrence to

Legal justification impossible.

sin; which expression he is bound to make, but is allowed to make without penalty when he may, does in fact make in the suffering of Christ; for this suffering is only so far in the nature of penalty as to yield the requisite equal expression of abhorrence. The law is satisfied, not by a substitution of suffering for suffering, but of one expression of abhorrence for another; allowing thus, it is imagined, a large economy in the penalty to be exacted. The invention is rather ingenious, but has no complexion of authority in the Scripture. Whatever may be thought of it, the problem it undertakes is so far the same as the satisfaction scheme proposes; viz., to find how a legal justification could be, and was, provided.

Now this legal justification, coming in one way or the other, is completely made up, as we may see, be-

Justified before faith in this legal way.
fore all repentances; for the law is satisfied, the punishment accepted, either in its pains or its adequate expression of justice, and the sinner is, at least, so far justified, that his account stands even. He certainly is either justified or not, and it makes very little difference which; for if we imagine that he has only a *ground* of justification made ready, waiting the condition precedent of faith, there is no faith waited for in the ground as such, that can do any good. There is no transforming efficacy in the faith of any mere fact, and the more implicitly one believes in the ground, that is, in the even score of his transgression, the less likely is he to be concerned for any thing farther, or to be-

lieve in any thing better. Is not justice satisfied? is not the law satisfied? What concern then shall he have for these, when they are in fact gone by, and never can be set up again for uses and retributive proceedings in any future time or world? What is wanted now is no mere credence for a fact, but a faith that is faith, and the ground so called is only a hindrance or impediment. For the faith that is faith will believe, not in that, but in a person; viz., Christ the righteous, passing over the soul to him. It is such a faith as yields the soul trustfully up to his pure life and all-transforming grace of sacrifice, and such, in that manner, as becomes a new-sprung life in the righteousness of God. But such a faith the supposed ground does not meet or match; one is not for the other; and if the transgressor imagines that he is justified on the score of the ground, he might as well be justified before the faith as after it, for the ground only helps him to be at peace in his sins, and his faith in the ground still leaves him there.

It is another fault of this legally grounded justification that it consents by definition to a really appalling fiction, proposing to justify or pass the subject, not as being just, but as if he were just, when confessedly he is not. Which makes the justification only so far real that it excuses the law, when it does not excuse or any way approve the man. Or if the man himself is justified, as we continually hear, and not the law excused, there is then no longer any place left for forgiveness. Indeed

The appalling fiction.

the man himself would take a singular liberty, in asking God's forgiveness for what he has already justified. We find him stranded thus in fact between two fictions; a forgiveness that has no opportunity, and a justification that has no truth. Is it any wonder, when a double fiction is thus let in at the center point of our gospel, there should be some lack of integrity in the life and practice of its disciples?

And there is yet another fiction set upon the doctrine, before it is finished, that is even worse and farther off from any real truth. As it is agreed that the law requires a perfect righteousness, nothing is justification which does not bring the perfect righteousness. Then it follows, the theologians tell us, that any thing is to be considered a righteousness which answers the demand of the law, and as Christ suffers in penalty what exactly answers the law, he is fairly said to provide us a righteousness. And then, if we look into the righteousness so called to find what is in it, we discover that the term *a righteousness* means no righteousness at all, but only that Christ contributes penal suffering enough to make us free of the law under sin, even as if we had not sinned, or were perfectly righteous. So far it is just as good as a righteousness, but, alas! how little does that mean! Our fall, our loss of righteousness, our dreadful hell of character—over this we are now allowed to lay the plaster called *a* righteousness! A righteousness that is in fact mere suffering, and as far as the mode of the fact is concerned, has

<small>Another fiction.</small>

nothing to do with righteousness at all, but only with providing a way of safety for unrighteousness. A theologic invention more dreadful than this, it is difficult to conceive. It was not invented as a fraud—I have no such thought—but the integrities of righteous living are of necessity broken and badly corrupted by it. It is a gospel which represents a mere pay-bill in penal suffering, set forth and commanded to be preached as being an actual gift of righteousness. If it seems to be a ground for hypocrisy instead of justification, the intention we are sure is not as bad as the look.

It is only an extension of the charges I am making in this line that the christian state of justification, when based in the faith of a mere legal satisfaction for sin, is a really ignoble matter in the experience, sordid and low in its motive, rising scarcely, if at all above the level of a jail-delivery transaction. *The justification itself is ignoble.* The transgressor has learned that his penal account is made even. Whereupon he congratulates himself that he is now safe, and need no more be troubled in his confidence; for the justification Christ has bought for him before the law, makes him free of the law, and what more can he want? His faith is in a mere political law-work that he has taken for his gospel, and has nothing in it that belongs to the noble confidence of justification in its true christian idea. For to be "made righteous" in the righteousness of God, which Christ declared by his death, is to receive him in such manner, by faith in his person, as to let in the inspiration force of his transcendent life and character; a matter how different, how grandly free, how unselfishly great, lifting the human experience up into ranges how consciously divine. I do not say, be it observed, that where the justified man supposes and believes in a doctrine of satisfaction rigidly legal, his experience will of course be graded as low as his doctrine. He will have sentiments often that are less prudential than his faith, and will be more frequently quickened by the righteousness of God than he ought to be. I only say that his doctrine itself ranges low, and, as far as it operates, will have a chilling and degrading effect in his experience. His legal justification state is bad, working only incapacity and detention.

Rehearsing these objections to any and all schemes of legal justification, it is a most happy sign for my doctrine, in the chapters on Propitiation and The Law, that they make room for no such doctrine, and leave us no conceivable want of it. By the law, as there conceived, we are only held in terms of penal discipline and not of desert or vindicatory justice, and the discipline is satisfied never, save when it is fulfilled, or consummated in a character deifically righteous. As the trial goes on we suffer scorches of law, and twinges of condemnatory pain, but our lacerations are measured by no principle of desert. They are not meant for justice, but to work conjunctively always with revelations of goodness and love concerned to win our obedience. These revelations in the cross and its arguments of mercy, do not undertake to master the law for us and pluck us out of its hands, as if it were a beast of prey, but they join hands with it, and give it welcome as a power working with them, in the same regenerative purpose, even when it worketh chastisement. All thoughts of a legal justification are, in this view, out of place, we can make no account of it. The wrath to come is by supposition yet future, and the dispensation of justice is not yet arrived. Nothing penal mixes with our discipline, only so far as it will help our recovery. Of course there will be scars of wrong defacing us, poisons of disease circulating through us, disproportions and disorders stealing in, so that if we pass out of life unconformed to God, these will be carried on as bad causations with us, to begin the new state of justice. And it will be a state emphatically new, making distributions henceforth in the scale of desert. For such a state there is of course no justification there. Only the bad causations can be called off here and taken quite away by what is fitly called "the justification of life;" that which heals all scars, extracts all poisons, tunes all discords and disorders in harmony, because it is a being entered into the righteousness of God, where the soul is new-charactered in the life and character of God.

I.

Thus far I have been occupied mainly with matters negative. I now pass on to verify the doctrine already vindicated, and very plainly asserted in the passage from the epistle to the Romans, at which this discussion began; viz., *that the true christian justification is that which makes righteous.*

If Christianity, or the christian Scripture, has any thing to boast, it is that it proves its grand superiority, and shows the manifest seal of God's inspirations, in having given to the world far back, in advance of all other literature, this most noble, stately, intellectually massive name for character; viz., RIGHTEOUSNESS. We have other words in the scripture and out of the scripture, built on different symbols, that answer well many of the requisite uses of morality or moral obligation, and sometimes of religion, but none that carry the distinctions of character with equal force and sharpness. *Law* is a word more nearly political and parliamentary, and better for a legal virtue than a free. *Obedience* supposes some other nature in a superior relation of authority, which leaves no room, save by a large accommodation, for its application to God. *Justice* [Latin, *justitia*] was even a more favorite moral word than *rectitudo* among the Romans because of their intensely legal character, but the forensic and judicial habit of the word associates always a false element, when it is applied to moral uses. *Goodness* is a word truly divine, when used by one who is in a spiritual habit, but it will be observed that unreligious minds are always sinking it to things done with generosity only, or out of a merely kind disposition. *Love* is the popular word of scripture obligation, partly because it has the disadvantage of being only a word of the affections,

Consider the word righteous.

demanding always some intellectual word to sharpen its applications, and be a regulative standard of its measures, times, and occasions. Higher than all these, and least ambiguous, and sharpest in the moral ring of it, is *right* or *righteousness*. The other flags require holding, all of them, but this can hold itself. A right line is the most inflexible of all symbols, and having this central image of necessary meaning in it, corrupt uses can not warp it; still it stands to its integrity as the plainly divine, visibly eternal word for character; declaring with Solomon, "Let thine eyes look right on, and thine eyelids look straight before thee;"* where—it may not be amiss to mention the fact—this word *straight* is represented in the Septuagint by the Greek word *dikaia*. What then but a first interest plainly of the world does Christ fulfill, in "declaring" by his death "the righteousness of God?"

We think it may be that we are just now coming at the fuller and more complete ethical development of this word right, having it for our conclusion, scientifically fixed and generally accepted, that moral obligation is grounded psychologically in the one necessary idea, or absolute law, of right; a conclusion which, whether we observe it or not, only brings out our supposed science upon the old scripture standard, which resolves all true character into right living, or righteousness. We can see too for ourselves what immense advances of thought have been made in this

---

* Prov iv, 25.

direction, by simply adverting to the times of Plato
and the studies of right, or justice,
which he and his Great Master have
given us. "Justice" [*dikaiosunē*] "is the virtue of
the soul," he says, "injustice the vice. The just soul
then and the just man will live well."* Speaking
also from his merely conscious experience, and not by
speculation, he reports a certain harmonic order in
the soul, when it is in righteousness, as if there were
some hidden tuning power in it, producing "a correct
arrangement of the parts towards each other, or about
each other." But when he comes to the reporting of
Socrates in his scientific debate of right or justice,
he reports him frankly confessing that he is strangely
mystified, or even balked by the problem. This
autocratic, all-piercing, indivertible idea, coming down
upon all mind and making all thought quiver to its
touch, whence comes it? and what is it? and whither
is it going? "Well," he says, "my excellent friend, if
all this be true I still want to know what is justice
[*i. e. right*]. Thereupon they think that I ask tiresome
questions, and am leaping over the barriers, and have
been already sufficiently answered, and they try to
satisfy me with one question after another, and at
length they quarrel. 'For one of them says that
justice is the sun [sun of righteousness?] and that he
only is the piercing or burning element which is the
guardian of nature. And when I joyfully repeat this
beautiful notion, I am answered by the satirical

---
* Republic Lib. I., Cap. xxiv.

[marginal note: Plato reporting Socrates.]

remark: 'What! is there no justice in the world, when the sun is down?' And when I earnestly beg my questioner to tell me his own honest opinion, he says, 'Fire in the abstract;' but that is not very intelligible. Another says, 'No, not fire in the abstract, but the abstraction of heat in the fire.' Another man professes to laugh at all this, and says, with Anaxagoras, that justice is soul [whose?] for soul, has absolute power, and mixes with nothing, and orders all things, and passes through all things. At last, my friend, I find myself in greater perplexity about justice [right] than I was before I began to learn."*

Dear great Master, how far off is he in these affecting mystifications, and half-worshipful homages, from any solution of this mighty word! Only this is clear, that he finds no reference in it to judicial analogies. What appears to almost take away his breath is the deific mystery of emphasis in it; commanding from behind all curtains *Psychological results.* and pillars of the creation; a causality every where hid, yet every where visible; the sun that makes internal witness night and day; fire without combustion always felt; mind undiscovered but pronouncing itself in the silences of thought; a mystery to be always debated, and yet in deepest amazement obeyed! Truly these two thousand years and more of debate have brought us over long reaches of distance, to settle us on the basis of morality we now commonly

---

* Cratylus.

think we have established; viz., everlasting right; a mere idea, that, in being simply thought, gets authority to command the world!

And yet all these advances were practically, though not psychologically, given us, full another thousand or fifteen hundred years before the time of Socrates himself, by the word of our ancient scripture. Far back of Plato and the Greek philosophy, back of the seige of Troy, back of the story of the Argonauts, either back of the times, or in the times, when the Aryan tribes and Vedic singers were pasturing their cows on the plains of the East Country, our Bible scripture shows us Abraham, the grand herdsman father, expostulating sharply with God, as if citing the categorical imperative to soften his undue severity—"Shall not the Judge of all the earth do right?"* However we can see a little way back, that Abraham is not talking here in the strain at all of the school ethics, but more as if the softening touch of some divine evangelism were upon him. He has come forth, as we see, out of the Chaldee country, leavened with a more than moral, a grandly religious training in the Righteousness of God. Others too are in the same, for he finds in the New West a priest of the Most High God, Melchizedek, whose very name shows that he is called by his countrymen, after the principle itself of the religion he ministers, *Melchizedek, i. e.*, King of Righteousness.† And then, as if to signify that he is in the secret,

^{Abraham before Socrates.}

---

* Gen. xviii, 25. † Gen. xiv, 18.

whether he knows it or not, of some divine evangelism going before upon him, he is put down as the King of Salem too; that is, King of Peace; where we find him in the very same conjunction of ideas that belong to christian justification. And the people and prophets coming after, warm their souls in the same; as Isaiah, for example, when he writes—" And the work of righteousness shall be peace ; and the effect of righteousness, quietness and assurance forever."* Which conjunction again is noted as a properly christian coincidence by the Epistle to the Hebrews— " First being by interpretation king of righteousness, and after that also king of Salem, which is king of peace." Now this may seem to be altogether fanciful, as every thing said of Melchizedek is wont to be; but, observe, I say not a word of the person of Melchizedek, as to who he is, or whence he comes, or what his relations to the christian future may be—for it really makes no difference whatever—I simply find the two words that are elemental in the experience of justification set religiously together somehow, it matters not how, and upon that fact I hang the conclusion that righteousness is already become the word for holy character. Abraham brought it from the East, and found it also in the West. And if now we add, what will by and by appear more fully and partly as an article of reason, that the being made righteous in the righteousness of God, is a truth as old as the world, and applicable to all moral natures in

---

* Isaiah xxxii, 17.

it, we shall have how little reason left to apprehend something fanciful in this conjunction of words, that we know we find among our antiquities, and that bring us out their ideas in the easy way of silence, and covertly as it were from themselves. It will not appear that there is any such putting forward of righteousness as a standard of character, in the nearly contemporary literature of the Aryan people, which, if it be as old as our scripture, or even older, has no name or definite conception for God, and which I do not find, by my restricted and rather second-hand knowledge, to have any rugged and rigidly determinate notion of duty, such as we name by the word righteousness.

But our scripture revelation does not stop in the antiquities of Genesis; but marks two other great advances to be distinctly noted. In the first it shows all holy character in men to be a grace derivative from the righteousness of God. Thus we have the Psalmist singing out his blessed promise even before the days of Homer—"He shall receive the blessing from the Lord, and righteousness from the God of his salvation."* And the prophets coming after echo and re-echo the same inspiring hope; one protesting "This is the heritage of the servants of the Lord, and their righteousness is of me, saith the Lord;"† and again, "he hath covered me with the robe of righteousness; for as the garden causeth the things

_{God declared as the spring of righteousness in men.}

---

* Psalms xxiv, 5. † Isaiah liv, 17.

that are in it to spring forth, so the Lord will cause righteousness and praise to spring forth before all nations;"* another, by a certain unmatched boldness of thought that comprehends all that is highest in God as the eternal source and fund of character, declaring, "this is the name whereby he shall be called, THE LORD OUR RIGHTEOUSNESS;"† another declaring Christ in his grand prerogative as Redeemer—"and to make reconciliation for iniquity and to bring in everlasting righteousness."‡ These wonderful scriptures, presenting God as the causative power of righteousness in all mortal natures, have only a sound of unmeaning jingle, I know, to many; the repetition of them does not even move respect. And the reason is that we have put them for long ages to a theologic use so mechanical and hollow that the living sense of them is dead. God undertakes in them, how visibly, to kindle the hope in us of a glorious new character from himself—which we, alas, conceive only to mean that he has bought us off from the punishment of our sins!—having provided us *a* righteousness.

Descending to the New Testament, we have the Saviour himself testifying in his very first sermon—"Blessed are they that hunger and thirst after righteousness for they shall be filled."§ He does not say, observe, they that hunger and thirst after *a* righteousness, but after righteousness. And again he declares at this earliest moment of his ministry—"Seek ye first the kingdom of God and his righteous-

---

* Isaiah lxi, 10, 11.   † Jer. xxiii, 6.   ‡ Dan. ix, 24.   § Matth. v, 6.

ness."* A most bold thought to put in any mortal mind that it is to seek the righteousness itself of God! Accordingly his new dispensation is called the ministration of righteousness,† and that, too, plainly in the sense of justification, because it antagonizes and quells, when embraced, the ministration of condemnation. To the same point comes another declaration; that "now the righteousness of God without the law is manifested, being witnessed by the law and the prophets, even the righteousness of God which is by faith of Jesus Christ unto all and upon all them that believe."‡ It is not, observe, a grace of penal suffering for, but a grace of righteousness *unto* and *upon* all them that believe. Hence the call of our salvation is "to yield our members instruments of righteousness unto God,"§ as if nothing now were necessary to put us fully in God's character but to yield our whole nature believingly up to his all-transforming righteousness. Thus when God has all our faculties offered up together to the harmonizing power of his righteousness, and to inspired co-working with it, they will be instruments discoursing only music from that time forth.

What I am here advancing then under this head is the fact of a grand stock character in God, that has been and is to be forevermore the spring of all character in his believing people. Thus it was long before any one ever had a thought of the possible satisfying of God's law and justice, by a contribution of

---

* Matth. vi, 33. † 2 Cor. iii, 9. ‡ Rom. iii, 21–22. § Rom. vi, 13.

pains to fill the legal quota of transgression, that Abraham, believing God in the promise of an heir, had the faith counted unto him for righteousness. Simply because every one brought home to God in such a way of faith, passes into God, so to speak, and is hid and covered and charactered in all action by his righteousness.

But a higher, finer point is finally reached, or finally will be, in the scripture development of this ideal standard. We are not only to have our righteousness derivatively from God, but God himself, as being its eternal source, will be in it, after a standard more perfect than we, to this hour, have commonly been able to imagine. How seldom do we think it requires any thing above justice and equity and fair consideration. Whereas God would not be right or righteous to himself, if he could think it less than wrong to not make cost, or endure even a cross for his enemy. Hence the representation that his Son is set forth to be a propitiation, because righteousness or right conviction—the eternal law before government —required it of him. Whence it follows, in a reverse order, that the blood and sacrifice of his Son declare "the righteousness of God in the forgiveness of sins." All this "that he may be righteous," not *just* in the retributive sense as our version is supposed to represent, "but righteous"—and have it seen that for righteousness' sake, he will forgive at bloody cost; so to new-character in righteousness him that believeth in

God's righteousness and that of the market, different.

Jesus. And how beautifully is the conception borne out, in the words of apostolic epithet under which he is presented—"*Jesus Christ the righteous.*"* He is called *the* righteous, observe, as if this were somehow the most emphatic and principally distinctive designation of his person. And that the epithet is used with a deliberate reference to the cross and the sacrifice for sin, is plainly seen from the words preceding; " we have an advocate with the Father;" as if he were "*the* righteous " in that very grace itself. The same thing also we have once more in the same epistle— " he is faithful and just," [that is righteous] " to forgive us our sins." Where the unhappy translation, *just*, really mocks the significance of the words; for who will imagine that God is faithful to forgive sins because he is forensically just? What, in fact, are we shown all the while with so great stress of misbegotten argument, as that God can not forgive sins without something done to satisfy his justice and take it out of the way? Here then it is that we behold the sublime peak of obligation where true righteousness culminates; viz., that it is to be fulfilled, and can be, only by sacrifice. Righteousness and sacrifice are even relative ideas. That Christ himself had this impression is sufficiently clear from his promise of the Spirit coming to reprove the world of righteousness, because his death will have taken him home now to the Father to be seen no more. The pure, great image of the righteousness of God, will now be discovered

---

* 1 John ii, 1.

in his reascension to the Father, showing plainly that he is not a being of this world.

How different a matter now is the justification that comes of justice satisfied, from this overspreading, all-assuring character in the righteousness of God. One believes in the cold-iron click of the turnkey open- Legal justification cold and poor. ing his door; the other in the sunrise and the soft-glowing, free-breathing radiance of the morning—always to rise and glow and breathe and be fresh morning for the soul's high liberty. And how strongly cast the contrast is we all discover, in the shock of incongruity it gives us to simply substitute justice for righteousness in the scripture uses. We can not read "sacrifices of justice"—"justice from the God of his salvation"—"the Lord our justice"—"Blessed are they that hunger and thirst after justice for they shall be filled"—"so by the justice of one the free gift came on all"—"the justice of God which is by faith of Jesus Christ unto all and upon all them that believe"—"much more doth the ministration of justice exceed in glory"—"new heavens and new earth wherein dwelleth justice;" indeed there is scarcely a passage, I know not one, in the Old and New Testament, that will not groan almost audibly when the word justice is stuck upon it as the synonym of righteousness. So clear it is that any proper and true justification is a state renewed in righteousness—that and nothing else.

Two other points concerning justification still remain, the presentation of which could not well be intermixed with the largely scriptural and verbal discussion of its nature just now closed. And first of all it needs to be observed, in order to a full understanding of justification, that it comes in the divine idea not after sin as a fact or condition previous, but was to be unconditionally every where and forever. For according to the original normal state of being, God was to be a power all diffusive, a central, self-radiating orb—Sun itself of Righteousness, shining abroad on all created minds and overspreading them with the sovereign day of its own excellence. The plan never was that created beings should be righteous, in such a sense, by their own works, or their own inherent force, as not to be derivatively righteous and by faith. They had and were eternally to have, their righteousness in God. Remaining upright, they would consciously have had their righteousness in God's inspirations, and would have been disturbed by a contrary suggestion.

Hence the dismal incapacity of sin; because it separates the soul from God's life-giving character and inspirations. Having Him no more, as the fontal source of righteousness, it falls off into an abnormal, self-centered state, where it comes under mere self-interest, and struggles vainly, if at all, in the tangle of that kind of endeavor to recover itself to its own ideals. Works of the law, dead works carefully piled, will-works, works of supererogation, penances, alms, austerities of self-mortification—none of these, nor all of them, make out the needed righteousness. Still there is a felt deficiency, which the apostle calls "a coming short of the glory of God." Nothing will suffice for this, but to come back, finite to infinite, creature to Creator, and take derivatively what, in its nature, must be derivative; viz., the righteousness that was normally and forever to be, unto, and upon, all them that believe.

Here then is the grand renewing office and aim of the gospel of Christ. He comes to men groping in a state of separation from God, consciously not even with their own standards of good, and, what is more, consciously not able to be—self-condemned when they are trying most to justify themselves, and despairing the more, the more they endeavor to make themselves righteous by their own works—to such Christ comes forth, out of the righteousness of God, and also in the righteousness of God, that he may be the righteousness of God upon all them that believe, and are so brought close enough to him in their faith, to receive his inspirations. And this is the state of justification, not because some debt is made even, by the penal suffering of Christ, but because that normal connection with God is restored by his sacrifice, which permits the righteousness of God to renew its everlasting flow.

When I speak thus of the connection with God as being restored by the sacrifice of Christ, let me not be understood as meaning by the sacrifice, only what is tenderly sympathetic and submissive in Christ's death. I include all that is energetic, strong, and piercing; his warnings, the pressure of his discipline, all that is done, by his powerful ministry and doctrine, to save us from the wrath to come. His sacrifice is no mere suit or plaint of weakness, for the righteousness of God is in it. When the metallic ring of principle, or everlasting right, is heard in the distress and wail of the cross, the sacrifice becomes itself a sword of conviction, piercing irresistibly through the sinner, and causing him to quiver on the point by which he is fastened. Mere sympathy, as we commonly speak, is no great power; it must be somehow a tremendous sympathy, to have the true divine efficacy. Hence the glorious justifying efficacy of Christ; because the righteousness of God is declared in his sacrifice.

Again, secondly, a more deliberate statement of the relations of faith to justification appears to be demanded. Though the righteousness of God is declared and made to shine with its true divine lustre and glory by Christ, still the justification is not conceived to be an accomplished fact, as indeed it never can be, prior to faith in the subject. It is justification by faith and not without—" and the justifier of him that believeth in Jesus." What is this faith, and why is it necessary?

<small>Faith how related to justification.</small>

It is not the belief that Christ has come to even our account with justice; neither is it the belief that he has obtained a surplus merit, which is offered, over and above, as a positive righteousness, and set to our credit, if we will have it. Neither of the two is a fact, or at all credible anywise. Nor would both, if believed as mere facts, do any thing more for us than a belief in any other facts. Our sins do not fly away because we believe in a fact of any kind. We can even believe in all the historic facts of Christianity, as thousands do, without being any the more truly justified.

No, the real faith is this, and very little intelligence is required to see the necessity of it; viz., the trusting of one's self over, sinner to Saviour, to be in him, and of him, and new-charactered by him; because it is only in that way that the power of Christ gets opportunity to work. So the sinner is justified, and the justification is a most vital affair; "the justification of life." The true account Faith defined. of it is that Jesus, coming into the world, with all God's righteousness upon him, declaring it to guilty souls in all the manifold evidences of his life and passion, wins their faith, and by that faith they are connected again with the life of God, and filled and overspread with his righteousness. And there springs up, in this reconnection of the soul with God's righteousness, a perfect liberty and confidence; for it is no more trying to climb up into a righteous consciousness and confidence by itself, but it has the righteousness by derivation; flowing down upon it, into it, and through it, by the eternal permeation of God's Spirit. And just here it is that Christianity wins its triumph. It shows man how to be free in good, and makes it possible. The best that all other religions and moralities can do, is to institute a practice of works, and a climbing up into perfection by our own righteous deeds; but the gospel of Jesus comes to our relief, in showing us how to find righteousness, and have it as an eternal inspiration; "even the righteousness of God that is by the faith of Jesus Christ unto all and upon all them that believe."* In it we do not climb, but rest; we goad ourselves into no impossibilities, groan under no bondage that we can not lift; sink into no deep mires because we try to struggle out. We have a possible righteousness, because it is not ours but God's; Christ received by our faith, to be upon us and for us, all that we could wish to be for ourselves. This is the transcendent distinction, the practically sublime glory of our gospel, our great all-truth—Justification by Faith. Here is conquered the grandest of all problems, how to put confidence in the bosom of guilt, and settle a platform of virtue that shall make duty free and joyful under all conscious disabilities.

Here it was that Luther broke into ecstasy, and a great bewilderment of change that he could not, *Luther's great discovery of justification.* for the time, understand. He had been trying to be justified by works; that is, by fastings, penances, alms, vigils, wearing down the body under the load of his sins, and crying to God in his cell, day and night, for some de-

---

* Rom. iii, 22.

liverance that should ease the torment of his still and always self-condemning soul. A right word from Staupitz let him see the fool that he was—that Christ would take him because he was guilty, having died for him because he was guilty, and not because he was righteous. At that point broke in, what light and confidence! His emancipated soul burst off all its chains in a moment, and took, as it were, the range of heaven in its liberty. He was new himself, the world was new, the gospel was new. It had not entered into his heart to conceive the things that were freely given him of God, but now he has them all at once. Justification by faith, justification by faith— his great soul is full of it; he must preach it, he must fight for it, die for it, know nothing else.

In the inspiration of this truth it was, that his great career as a reformer and spiritual hero began. If any thing will make a man a hero, it will be the righteousness of God upon him, and the confidence he gets in the sense of it. If he can be eloquent for any thing, it will be *Luther's head did not understand his heart.* in the testimony of what Christ is to him, in the now glorified consciousness of his inward life. But we must not fall into a very great mistake here. Luther is, in fact, two, not one; viz., a Christian, and a theologian; and his Christian justification by faith, that which puts such a grand impulsion into his feeling, and raises the tone of his manhood to such a pitch of vigor, is a very different, altogether separate matter, from that theologic contriving of his head, which he took so confidently for the certain equivalent. Taking this latter, it would be difficult to find how any one should become much of a hero, or be lifted to the pitch of any great sentiment, in it. Indeed, the very great wonder is, that a man so intelligent should imagine, for a moment, that he was fired with a passion so mighty, and a joy so transcendent, by the fact that an innocent being had taken his sins, and evened the account of justice by suffering their punishment! This he thought he believed; but we are not obliged to believe that he did.* Really believing it, and conceiving what it means, the fact would have set his stout frame shuddering, and turned his life to gall. The truth indeed appears to be, that his heart sailed over his theology, and did not come down to see it. We find him contriving, in his "Epistle to the Galatians," how Christ, having all the sins of mankind imputed to him, "becomes the greatest transgressor, murderer, adulterer, thief, rebel, and blasphemer, that ever was, or could be, in all the world;" and his doctrine is, that suffering the just wrath of God, for the sin that is upon him, Christ makes out a right of justification for us before God, which is complete, because it completely satisfies the law. And then to be just cleared of punishment, and believe that he is, he conceives to be the very thing that makes his glorious liberty and raises the tempest of his joy! The manner appears to be hideous, the deliverance to be negative and legal only; but his heart is ranging high enough, in its better

---

* Note 4.

element—the righteousness of God—not to be offended by the crudities he is taking for a gospel.

But this is not the first time that the head of a great man has not been equal to the understanding, or true interpretation, of his heart. Indeed, nothing is more common, as a matter of fact, than for men of real or even the highest intelligence, to so far misinterpret their own experience in matters of religion, as to ascribe to it, and find it springing radically out of, that which has no sound verity, and could never have produced such an experience. Let no one be surprised, then, that Luther's justification by faith, that which puts his soul ringing with such an exultant and really sublime liberty, makes a plunge so bewildering into bathos and general unreason, when it comes to be affirmed theologically in his doctrine. As he had it in his Christian consciousness, the soul of his joy, the rest of his confidence, the enlargement of his gracious liberty, nothing could be more evidently real and related to the deepest realities of feeling; but as he gave it in his dogmatic record, I confess that calling it justification by faith—*articulus stantis, vel cadentis ecclesiæ*—I could more easily see the church fall than believe it. Happily our very great reverence and admiration for the man may be accommodated in the confidence that any one may reject it utterly, and yet receive all that his faith received in his justification; and may also be with him in profoundest sympathy, in the *magnificat* he chants, and, with such exhaustless eloquence of boasting, reiterates, in his preaching of the cross and the glorious liberty it brings. Certain it is that no man is a proper Christian, who is not practically, at least, in the power of this great truth. If any thing defines a Christian, it is that he is one who seeks and also finds his righteousness in God.

II.

I am well aware how insufficient this exposition of the great Christian truth, justification by faith, will be to many—to some, because it is a truth that can be sufficiently expounded by nothing but a living experience of its power; to others, because they have already learned to find their experience in words and forms of doctrine, by which it is poorly, or even falsely represented. What questions the view presented will encounter, especially from this latter class, I very well know, and will therefore bring the subject to a conclusion by answering a few of them.

Do we not then, by holding a view of justification so essentially subjective, virtually annihilate the distinction between justification and sanctification? This is one of the questions, and I answer it by saying that if the two experiences were more closely related than they are commonly supposed to be, I do not see that we need be greatly disturbed on that account. Still they are sufficiently distinct. According to the Catholic doctrine they are virtually identical; because the "making just," or "making righteous," which is con-

Justification and sanctification not confounded.

ceived to be the sense of justification, is understood to be a complete subjective change, one that goes below consciousness and makes the soul inherently right— which is the very significance also of sanctification. But if we only conceive the soul to be so joined, by its faith, to the righteousness of God, as to be rather invested by it, or enveloped in it, than to be transformed all through in its own inherent quality; if the righteousness goes on, even as the sun goes on shining when it makes the day, and stops of necessity when the faith withdrawn permits it to go on no longer; then we have a very wide and palpable distinction. The consciousness of the subject, in justification, is raised in its order, filled with the confidence of right, set free from the bondage of all fears and scruples of legality; but there is a vast realm back of the consciousness, or below it, which remains to be changed or sanctified, and never will be, except as a new habit is generated by time, and the better consciousness descending into the secret roots below, gets a healing into them more and more perfect. In this manner, one who is justified at once, can be sanctified only in time; and one who is completely justified is only incipiently sanctified; and one who has consciously "yielded his members as instruments of righteousness unto God," may discover even more and more distinctly, and, by manifold tokens, a law in his members not yet sanctified away. There is also a certain reference in justification to one's standing in everlasting principle; whereas sanctification refers more especially to the conscious purity of the soul's aims, and the separation of its moral habit from evil. By another distinction, justification is the purgation of the conscience, and sanctification a cleansing of the soul's affections and passions. Both of course are operated by God's inspirations, and are operated only in and through the faith of the subject.

There is indeed no objection to saying that, in a certain general way, they are one—just as faith is one with love, and love with regeneration, and this with genuine repentance, and all good states with all others. The same divine life or quickening in God is supposed in every sort of holy exercise, and the different names we give it represent real and important differences of meaning, accordingly as we consider the new life quickened in relation to our own agency, or to God's, or to means accepted, or trusts reposed, or effects wrought. In the same way, justification is sanctification, and both are faith; and yet their difference is by no means annihilated.

Another question likely to be raised in the way of objection is, whether, in the kind of justification stated, I do not give in to the rather antiquated notion of imputed righteousness? To this I answer, that if the notion supposed to be thus antiquated, is the theologic fiction of a surplus obedience, over and above what was due from Christ as a man—contributed by him in pains and acts of duty from the obedience of his higher nature—which surplus is imputed to us and reckoned to our

How related to imputation?

account, such imputation is plainly enough rejected; still there will be left the grand, experimental, Scripture truth of imputed righteousness, a truth never more to be antiquated than holiness itself.

The theologic fiction more fully stated appears to have been something like this: that Christ, taken simply as a man, was under all the obligations that belong to a man; therefore that he was only righteous as he should be in fulfilling those obligations, and had no righteousness to spare; but that, as being the God-man, he was under no such obligations; whence it resulted that, by his twofold obedience, passive and active, he gained two kinds of surplus righteousness; a passive to stand in the place of our punishment and be a complete satisfaction for it, and an active to be set to our account as being our positive obedience—both received by imputation. And so we are justified and saved by a double imputed righteousness, one to be our suffered penalty, the other to be such an obedience for us as will put us even with the precept of the law. It is even a sad office to recite the scholastic jingle of such a scheme, made up and received for a gospel. Plainly it is all a fiction. The distinction of a passive and active obedience is a fiction; the passive obedience being just as voluntary as the active, and therefore just as active. The assumption that Christ, to put righteousness upon us, must provide a spare righteousness not wanted for himself, is a fiction that excludes even the possible *koinonia* of the righteousness of God. And a still greater fiction is the totally impossible conception of a surplus righteousness. Christ was just as righteous as he should be, neither more nor less, and the beauty of his sacrifice lay in the fact, not that it overlapped the eternal law, but that it so exactly fulfilled that law. His merit therefore was not that he was better than he should be, but all that he should be; for if he was perfect without the surplus, then he was more than perfect with it, and we are left holding the opinion, that there is a righteousness above and outside of perfection! Still again the imputation of such a perfection to us, so that we shall have the credit of it, is a fiction also of the coldest, most unfructifying kind, and impossible even at that. What has any such pile of merit in Christ, be it suffering, or sacrifice, or punishment, or active righteousness, to do with my personal deserts? If a thousand worlds-full of the surplus had been provided for me, I should be none the less ill-deserving if I had the total reckoning in possession.

The experimental, never-to-be antiquated, Scripture truth of imputed righteousness, on the other hand, is this:—That the soul, when it is gained to faith, is brought back, according to the degree of faith, into its original, normal relation to God; to be invested in God's light, feeling, character—in one word, righteousness—and live derivatively from Him. It is not made righteous, in the sense of being set in a state of self-centered righteousness, to be maintained by an ability complete in the person, but it is made righteous in the sense of being always to be made righteous; just as the day is made luminous, not by the light of sunrise staying in it, or held fast by it, but by the ceaseless outflow of the solar effulgence. Considered in this view, the sinning man justified is never thought of as being, or to be, just in himself; but he is to be counted so, be so by imputation, because his faith holds him to a relation to God, where the sun of His righteousness will be forever gilding him with its fresh radiations. Thus Abraham believed God enough to become the friend of God—saying nothing of justice satisfied, nothing of surplus merit, nothing of Christ whatever —and it was imputed to him for righteousness. No soul comes into such a relation of trust, without having God's investment upon it; and whatever there may be in God's righteousness—love, truth, sacrifice —will be rightfully imputed, or counted to be in it, because, being united to Him, it will have them coming over derivatively from Him. Precisely here therefore, in this most sublimely practical of all truths, imputed righteousness, Christianity culminates. Here we have coming upon us, or upon our faith, all that we most want, whether for our confidence, or the complete deliverance and upraising of our guilty and dreadfully enthralled nature. Here we triumph. There is therefore now no condemnation, the law of the spirit of life in Christ Jesus hath made us free. If we had a righteousness of the law to work out, we should feel a dreadful captivity upon us. If we were put into the key of righteous living, and then, being so started, were left to keep the key ourselves, by manipulating our own thoughts, affections, actions, in a way of self-superintendence, the practice would be so artificial, so inherently weak, as to pitch us into utter despair in a single day. Nothing meets our want, but to have our life and righteousness in God, thus to be kept in liberty and victory always by our trust in Him. Calling this imputed righteousness, it is no conceit of theology, no fiction, but the grandest and most life-giving of all the Christian truths.

We have this imputation also in another form that is equally natural and practical. Thus, instead of having our faith imputed unto us for righteousness, we ourselves teach our faith to locate all our righteousness putatively in God; saying "The Lord our righteousness," "Christ who is our life," "made unto us righteousness;" as if the stock of our virtue, or holiness, were laid up for us in God. All the hope of our character that is to be, we place, not in the inherent good we are to work out, or become in ourselves, but in the capital stock that is funded for us in Him. And then the character, the righteousness, is the more dear to us, because it is to have so high a spring; and God is the more dear to us, that he will have us hang upon him by our faith, for a matter so divine. And the joy also, the confidence, the assurance and rest— all that we include in our justification—is the more sublimely dear, that we have it on a footing of permitted unity with God, so transforming and glorious.

We also to have our righteousness putatively in God.

There is, in short, no truth that is richer, and fuller of meaning and power, than this same figure of mental imputation, in which we behold our character laid up and funded for us in the righteousness of God. In one view it is not true; there is no such quantity, or substance, separate from him, and laid up in store for us; but there is a power in him everlastingly able to beget in us, or keep flowing over upon us, every gift our sin most needs; and this we represent to our hearts, by conceiving, in a figure, that we have a stock, just what we call "our righteousness," laid up for us, beforehand, in the richly funded stores of his eternity.

It is no fault then of our doctrine of justification by faith, that it favors a notion of imputed righteousness; for in just this fact it is, that the gospel takes us out of the bondage of works into a really new divine liberty. Here, in fact, is the grand triumph of Christianity; viz., in the new stage of righteousness inaugurated, which makes the footing of a sinner good, and helps the striving bondman of duty to be free; even the righteousness of God that is by faith of Jesus Christ, unto all, and upon all them that believe. When this is antiquated, just then also will salvation be.

CHAPTER IV.

THREEFOLD DOCTRINE OF CHRIST CONCERNING HIMSELF.

<small>A great omission of Christ regretted.</small>

It must have occurred to a great many disciples, working in the interest of doctrine, to imagine how great a thing it would have been, had Christ himself, in his own superior, unquestionable competence, seen fit to frame a statement for his followers of what he himself conceived his gospel, or the doctrine of his gospel, to be. It may even have been a subject of wonder, sometimes, that he did not do it. All the greater wonder, that he could have done it so easily, and saved, or at least greatly reduced, the necessity of misunderstandings and controversies often painful. And yet, if I rightly conceive his meaning, he has, in fact, done it; presenting us a complete and explicit summation of the results he will have accomplished by his life and death. For this appears to be the significance of what he puts forth in his promise of the Comforter.* His very design is, if I am right, to show us in this passage, the doctrinal outfit he will have provided for the Spirit, coming now to take his place. It is expedient, he

---

* John xvi. 7–15.

(218)

says, for him now, since he has done, as in terms of body and space, all which can be done under such limitations, to withdraw from visibility, or go away. In this kind of ministry having come to his limit, only by another can his work be fulfilled. A traveling grace can not, by supposition, be ecumenical. What is wanting now is a distributive power that can be present every where, and occupy all places, without travel or transition; a Spirit universal that has the liberty of the world. The new ministration of the Comforter, now promised, is to be exactly this; a Christ delocalized, invisible, under no laws of space, and practically universal. *He puts off now locality and form.*

Three things, in particular, are to be the outfit of his working in all the ages to come; which three things he now calls "the things that are mine;" because he has prepared them by his life and death, and gotten them ready, as in word and form, to be the instrumental forces of truth and spirit invisible or out of form—"He shall glorify me, he shall receive of mine, and shall show it unto you." They compose a creed, as he gives it, in three articles; for though he does not give them to be a creed in our sense of the term, he does give them to be a brief summation of what he has done, set forth in their potential value, or practical significance. He will go forth now, no more as in body, but as all-diffusive, every where present Spirit, reproving the world of sin, and of righteousness, and of judgment— *His three articles.*

"Of sin," he says, "because," being what I have been and doing what I have done, "they believe not on me." "Of righteousness because I go to the Father"—borne up in ascension to worlds above the world—"and ye see me no more." "Of judgment because the prince of this world is judged"—cast down, crushed and visibly brought under. In Christ's own opinion, as we see, these three things are the substance of what he has done for the world, the equipment he has made ready for the Spirit, and put in hand to be the operative force of his regenerative ministry for the world. In the use of this divine armament he becomes, what is here given to be his designation, the Spirit of truth; for the threefold substance of doctrine here set forth is to be his implemental power.

There really appears to be no word of scripture which has fared as badly, at the hands of preachers and commentators, as this word *Comforter*, of which I now speak. I say this considering the difficulty of finding any word in English that will fitly represent the Greek word *Paraclete*. It is once translated Advocate.* The commentators suggest other words such as *Helper, Counselor, Teacher, Intercessor*. The very poorest, thinnest representation ever proposed, or adopted, is our English name Comforter. And it is all the worse that it is evidently intended to be taken as being naturally descriptive; for another word is even

_{The word Comforter a mistake.}

---
* 1 John ii, 1.

palpably mistranslated to conform to it—" I will not leave you comfortless "*—where the word " comfortless " represents the word *orphans* in the original, the Saviour's design being in that word to say that he will not leave his disciples deserted, robbed of company and counsel; a very different matter from being left uncomforted. As if their being uncomfortable, or not sufficiently comforted, were a principal, or prominent concern of the Master; a friend whose dignity it was to hold the rational and manly view of all experience, and have it as a matter conceded, that the best thing for them will sometimes be to fall out of condition, and be as grandly superior to all self-sympathy in the loss of earthly comforts, as he has been himself. No, there is no such feeble, over-soft sympathy in the Saviour's mind, in this parting hour, that he should be contriving how especially to put his disciples in comfort and leave them so. Besides, his concern here is not for his disciples, but specially for such as he calls " the world ;" for it is the world he is going to convince and bring to righteousness. And if the Spirit to be given is to be a gift having special reference to this, which appears in the manner of the language, the name Comforter is a name wholly inappropriate. To be comforted is just the thing the world as such does not want. And the Saviour has a much heavier and nobler concern; viz., the organizing of a grace for the world, such as he is just now bringing to completion. He is

---

* John xiv, 18.

planning to unlocalize, universalize, and make victorious, the great salvation he has undertaken for mankind. And his idea stands on the face of the word he adopts for the designation of this promised ministry, whether we can find an English name for it or not. It is Paraclete—*Para near, klētos call*—the *Near-caller*, the *Bringer-in*, for salvation; a word in no soft, soothing key, but a bugle note of summons rather, such as the work of the Spirit, in the in-gathering and organizing of the everlasting kingdom, fitly requires.

As we strike this conception we begin to see how grand a thought is in the Saviour's mind when he names his three things. They are as far off, all, from the insipid offices of comfort as they can be, and are rightly named as reproving powers—"reproving of sin, of righteousness, of judgment—just such offices of truth, and piercing conviction, as the great Bringer-in of the world must needs fulfill.

At the same time I quite willingly concede that there is a certain superficial aspect of fairness, in the representations that interpret the promised Spirit by the words *Comforter* and *Comfort;* for it may be imagined, from the words "Whom the world can not receive,"* that the promise is to have its value in the experience only of disciples. But when construed in that way, the express terms of the threefold promise, in the sixteenth chapter, are even all of them denied any

<small>He dispenses comfort, of course.</small>

---

* John xiv, 17.

chance of meaning at all. Besides the grand effect is formally declared to be, in a "reproving of *the world*"—raising sentiments of conviction, sensibilities of character, impressions of judgment, in the world. And we are not required to run our interpretation directly against this passage by insisting that the other—" Whom the world can not receive "—must be taken in the largest meaning possible; for it probably means only that the world as world, unmoved, unreproved, dwelling wholly apart from God in the blindness of nature, can not thus receive or entertain the Spirit. Nothing is more affectingly true. Holding this view of the scripture in question, I am not required to say that the Holy Spirit of promise is to have no office of comfort included in his work. He is to fulfill every good office in his ministry, even as Christ himself did. But it will be as far as possible from any right statement of his mission, that he is to be, in chief and in a degree most of all significant, a dispenser of comfort. Christ's own last words in the inspiring strain of comfort and courage and patience under persecutions to come, are full of beauty and of tender cheer, but it is not proposed that the Holy Spirit should always or ever make that kind of comfort any principal object of his work. He will comfort where he may; convince, correct, fortify in patience, chasten, bring low, confound by rebuke, where he must.

Taking now this general view of the Spirit in Christ's three points above stated, there ought to be some light for us in them, if we go over them carefully and make up our conception from them, as we easily may, of the gospel doctrine designedly summarized in them. We shall get in this manner, a fresh coining of the gospel idea, clear of all the constructive wisdoms and unwisdoms heretofore propounded as the inevitable theologic truth. For this three-membered gospel, set off and labeled numerically for the outfit of the Spirit, appears to have scarcely taken the attention hitherto of the formularies and school functionaries. Wherefore it is left us, or appears to be, for our privilege, to draw first lessons here of atonement from the lips of Christ himself.

It may not be amiss to suggest, as a reason for this oversight, that the preachers and commentators appear to have been too much occupied with the stress Christ lays on the work of the Spirit, to observe, at all, the rather silent implication of his reference to the part he himself is to have in the work. It is not simply promised, we are to observe, that the Spirit will do these things, but that he will do them *in* and *by* the energizing powers of impression now made ready for his use. In the first it is as if it were said, "They shall look on me whom they have pierced." The conviction wrought by the Spirit is to come of what Christ has been to men, who yet do not believe in him. So of the "righteousness:" it shall be what Christ himself has revealed by his life and death and

Christ not to be overlooked here.

ascension to the Father. And the same is true as we shall see of the world reproved " of judgment." The Spirit will be the agent, Christ the power. We do but half conceive the Saviour when we refer all these three-fold results to the Spirit; for he works them, if at all, by a dispensing of Christ from the magazine stock He has furnished. In this view we now return to the threefold matter of the promise.

ARTICLE I. *Of sin because they believe not on me.* In recovering our fallen race to God, the first thing is to beget in them a fixed conviction of their fall, and the thraldom of their guilt, as creatures alienated from God. And this Christ thinks he is doing; for it is "the world" observe that he will thus reprove. His thought is, we can see, that from this time forth, as the result of his incarnate life and death, there is to be a new sensibility to sin, not only in individual persons, but in the world itself, such as never before was observed. I feel quite sure too that a sufficiently sharp investigation would show it to be so; that religious sentiments and convictions run deeper and carry more heat through mind, since Christ's day than before, in all the peoples that are in the knowledge of his cross. I recollect no instance of remorse, for example, in the literature and story of the Greeks, that holds any correspondence or comparison with examples that are even common in the Christian nations. And what is closely related, the sense of sin is sharper and more

<small>New sensibility to sin under Christ.</small>

heavily pronounced in the Christian peoples and literatures than elsewhere. Indeed, I might almost venture to say that there is no proper sense of sin outside of the gospel religion. There is sensibility enough to wrongs suffered, and a considerable sense of wrongs done. But these are sins only, not sin. The state of sin as a condition of life underlaid with guilt, infested with poisons, and become a second nature in the run of its bad causations, is a quite different matter. Only a very few of the first minds out of Christianity such as Plato, Seneca, and others, are observed to become distinctly conscious of sin, whereas in the saving work of the Spirit under Christ, no one, however humble or weak, is conceived to be in the possible range of a true conversion to God, who is not prepared to it by the conviction of sin as a state. No man is converted to a new life under the consciousness of a sin, or this, or that, or even many sins, unless there is implicitly joined with that consciousness, or included in it, the sense of a guiltiness that is chronic and by the subject himself incurable. Hence the Saviour says "of sin," well understanding that it is sin he is required to cure, and not sins that he has undertaken to simply correct. And, in order to this, some plummet of reproving, deep enough to reach the bottom of the sea, needs to be let down in guilty bosoms, and make report to them of what is commonly hid in the ooze that underlies their consciousness. It is remarkable in this view that the appalling chapters of reproof and judgment,

Sins, not sin, commonly felt.

which occur in the world's history before the crucifixion scene of Christ's death, almost none of them strike deep enough to plough up and set in true conviction the radical fact of sin, as distinguished from particular sins. Is there not some reason to doubt the possibility of doing more, until the moral consciousness of the race may be made capable of it by ages of discipline?

Hence the flood, in whatever degree of universality we conceive it, was not so much God's argument with sin, as his act of extirpation, washing the world clean of it. However, it has had a valuable efficacy doubtless ever since, as a witness of the divine displeasure against the ways of license and revolting wickedness. The fire-blast that fell on Sodom and Gomorrah, and the earthquake shock that swallowed them, have been used in all ages since, as appeals of warning. We ourselves have many times heard such appeals, and their fiery terrors we have seen chasing guilty souls up out of the plain into the mountains of refuge, till we have sometimes doubted whether more of hurry and panic than of true conviction, is not sometimes instigated by them. No one doubts that alarm may sometimes be stronger than consideration, and that when it is, more of damage will follow than of benefit. In the giving of the law at the foot of the thundering, smoking mount, an impression of God's authority was made by the sceneries of the occasion, that must of course intensify the dread of sin, though it may not have had

Defects of the old methods.

any great effect in awakening the consciousness of it. And there was the less reason to expect any such result, in the fact that the statutes of the law refer only to sins of particular action, and not to the state of sin itself as a matter of much deeper concern. The same thing is to be said commonly of the stinging reproofs, and fiery rebukes, hurled at the sins of the time by the old preachers of Israel, in what was called their prophesying. They shot point blank every time, and kept the air ringing with specific and particular charges, which gave them a sufficiently pungent ministry, but they could not move the deeps of character and conviction, as they would have done had they been able to speak more reflectively, threading the sensibilities back of the sins, and blazing their torches in the caverns of the soul where sin itself is hid. About the most impressive exhibition of sensibility to sin, which occurs any where in the times previous to Christ's coming, is shown us in the scene that follows the discovery of the book of the law.* Partly because of the tenderness produced by a mental retroversion, that imagines how the wrath of the Lord must be kindled by the neglects of the fathers, "not hearkening to the words of the book," but allowing it to be lost among the lumber of the temple chamber. It is felt now as the public sin, a kind of original sin, that has been running down through long ages and generations gone by. The whole people were deluged thus with guiltiness coming down upon

---

* 2 Kings xxii. 8, et seq.

them in the line of their family blood and affections, and the king rent his clothes in their midst, and wept before the Lord.

I sketch this outline simply to show how difficult a thing it is to raise a true sensibility to sin, such as that which made itself evident in the time of the Pentecost shortly after Christ's ascension. *How Christ himself reproves.* And this scene of the Pentecost was a kind of first-stage proof of Christ's meaning when he said, "Of sin because they believe not on me." His understanding was, in these words, that he was going by his death to move on the hardness and blindness of transgression, by a comparatively new method, giving us, in that fact, the first article of his gospel. He is not going to shake the security of sin by terrors of any kind. He will paint no sceneries of wrath on the sky. He will not arraign, or reprove, or denounce more pungently than was ever done before. He will have simply proved himself to be the friend of man, by the sublimest and most disinterested charities and a character so great all round as to be more than mortal, and beside this will have done nothing to so much as remind men of their sin. Only being such in the worth and more than human beauty of his life, he will simply let the wrong that is in guilty bosoms break itself upon his silence, and prove what is in it by its act of murder! And not even the murder is to implicate more than a very few persons. Only the race, looking on, will confess, "these were men, our fellow men," as all the people did who came together to that sight, and beholding the things which were done, without being active in them, smote their breasts and returned. Here, now, is another way of reproving that cuts the world clean through. Every man sees what is in man—in himself—by the impatience that could be mortally exasperated by goodness, and rush upon the Son of God himself in a deed of murder. And the conviction thus wrought is no dry hammer-stroke under the law, of which we sometimes hear, but it has a quality more personal than legal, running fluid in the form as all personal feeling will; a new-born, silent, all-pervading sensibility to sin, such as Christ himself expected. Furthermore, it is not stated in a way to magnify the flagrance of bad action as a positive ill-doing, but the sin is to be revealed to itself in what it does not, rather than in what it does. "Of sin because they believe not on me;" for the not believing is itself a token how significant, when a grace so beautiful and grandly impressive is revealed. And what, in fact, is the proof most appalling of the sin-state of the world, but that it can look on so great glory and still not believe?

Neither is it any answer, at this point, that not believing is no crime, because we are under no obligations to believe. For man is made to be a believing creature as truly as a reasoning creature. He is even to apprehend the highest reaches of truth and being, by believing what belongs to faith, and can no otherwise be received.

<small>Guilt revealed by unbelief.</small>

So that when he lives in a way to never behold the greatest and most captivating realities crowded on his faith, he lives below himself, "alienated from the life of God by the ignorance that is in him because of the blindness of his heart." Indeed, the sin of sin is more than any thing else, in the not believing of what is best revealed, most credible and holiest to be received. Even as the great assembly of the Pentecost began to feel when the guilt of their unbelief, displayed in the scene of the cross, began to be judgment revealed by the preaching of Peter. And so that word—"Of sin because they believe not on me," has been fulfilled in its power from that day to this.

ARTICLE II. *Of righteousness because I go to the Father and ye see me no more."* The statement here made is condensed to the last degree, but I think we can not miss the idea. Christ is not any the more truly righteous, as we all can see, that he dies and goes home to the Father, to be seen no more. But, being as truly righteous, we can, beyond a question, far better appreciate his righteousness after he is gone, than we could if he still remained with us.

All great excellence and transcendent worth of character are partly unappreciated, till they are seen to be consummated in the article of death. *Removal consummates great character.* Many hard accusations doubtless fell on Enoch, before the day when "he was not, because God took him." Moses was how often chidden and rebelled against, and never measured in the greatness of his worth, till God called him up into Nebo to die, and buried him there himself, in a place that only he shall ever know. Socrates was charged with many crimes, and especially with corrupting the youth, and refusing due honors to the gods of his people. But when he took the fatal cup, refusing, as a matter of supreme duty to the state, to accept the chance of flight provided by his friends, what was there left for his people, but to turn his sentence back on the life of his chief accuser, drive his conspirators into exile, and raise a statue to him as the righteous man, out of their own hearts' devotion. Aristides had been called the *Just*, that is the righteous, till some of the people had become quite tired of it. Finally, after having proved his capacity many times over as one of the greatest commanders of his country, and his title as the Just a great many times more, by acts and arbitration judgments bearing the stamp of his wonderful uprightness, he became extremely old, growing all the while more cheap in his virtue as he grew more customary in it, and finally fell out of life and his many public offices and trusts, as a man almost forgotten by his people. But when they heard of his sublime poverty—that he could only be buried at the public expense—they woke up, as it were, at the discovery of so great public honor and fidelity, and found no way possible to pay their debt but by lavishing thus late on his family, rewards that were due them only as bearing his name.

Now these humble, merely human examples fall a

great way short, I know, of the case for which they are cited, but they let us in very deep nevertheless into the secret of the Saviour's meaning when he says—"Of righteousness because I go to the Father and ye see me no more." He understands that when he is gone, ascended to the Father in a way so impressive, a great revision will commence, and a great discovery will be made. He had come down out of the righteousness of God in his advent, he had given it for beatitude to his followers to be "hungering and thirsting after righteousness" —"seeking first the righteousness of God"—he had been himself a remarkable man in his life, sufficiently remarkable to be considered a prophet; yet one thing more he still perceives is wanting before his followers will begin to imagine the deific property in his character; he must go back into God as he came forth out of God, and when his death and reascension have taken him quite away, great revisions of thought will come, and the true deific righteousness will begin to beam out upon them, and the unmatched glory of his nature will be fully discovered. Discovery most transcendently blessed and powerful, how shall they name it but to say—The Lord Our Righteousness!

Christ counts on a great revision.

There has never entered into human thought before, any so pure image of good, any so glorious conception of the righteous in character. Men had framed high thoughts before of the abstract righteousness of God. Now they have it dewed with personality, exampled and offered in terms of human life and sympathy. God is not greater of course in his righteousness than before, but the manly voice and bearing, and the well-doing and well-suffering, have made him closer, more congenially, powerfully great. And Christ does not conceal it from us that, in this matter of the righteousness to be discovered in his departure, he expects to have a warmth and glory added that will make his life a seminally quickening force in unbelieving minds—a reproving that will be the living impression of righteousness. And his expectation is abundantly justified. It has not only operated as a new creative force in multitudes without number, of guilty, morally fallen men, but it has leavened the general mass of Christendom with a sensibility to character before unknown. Men hear a Christly accent in principles, perhaps without knowing it, and love, and truth, and equity, in one word righteousness, holds a closer and more tender proximity than ever before. And the explanation of it is in what the Saviour says—"He shall reprove the world of righteousness, because I go to the Father and ye see me no more."

The new begotten sense of character.

I will only add that there is a very great importance in this Second Article, in the fact that it yields an inference so conclusive against the paymaster scheme of justification. And it is the more conclusive that nothing is ad-

No legal justification here.

vanced antagonistically, but only in a simple way of promise and hope for righteousness. There is no legal substitution named or even thought of by Christ, as that having satisfied the law by suffering, he has bought a complete legal righteousness and so has laid a ground of justification. His reproving of righteousness is to be a quickened sensibility for righteousness itself, and a new capacity of great character thus prepared—that and nothing more. And if he had been asked whether he expected to buy a new righteousness for us by his cross, and have it put to our account, so that we can be justified and delivered of our sins, I really do not think he would have understood or conceived so much of theology. No, by his reproving of righteousness he simply means that he will put us in the power and occupancy of it; which he will do by the revealed image given us of it in his life and suffering; without thrusting us into any of the speculative and scholastic subtleties that have since been the annoyance of his people. Having first, by the loving sacrifice of his death, reproved the unbelieving of their sin, he next finds how to impress their sin with the manifested glory of righteousness—giving them a new sensibility for both, one as malady and the other as cure—knowing well that when our thought gathers to his reascended person, considering again what the true glory hid in his descended person was, it will be as if the spaces between us and God were bridged, and his righteousness were now with us and upon us. For it is in fact the righteousness of God declared or shown, that we may be made righteous in it, as Paul himself explicitly teaches. In the simplest possible form of conceiving it, "Christ is made unto us righteousness." Or the same thing is said in other words equally plain—"That we might be the righteousness of God in him." And it is beautiful to see how Luther, in his comment on this reproving of righteousness, drops out his litigiousness and his scholastic legalities of justification, to speak of the overspreading, inwardly transforming righteousness, as if that in fact were all. Thus, chanting as it were his hymn, he says—"Now he did not go thus to the Father for his own sake; but, as he came for our sakes from heaven, and became our flesh and blood, so for our sakes he went up again, after he had completed the victory over sin, death, and hell, and entered into that government, whereby he delivers us from all these, and rules in such manner that his kingdom is called, and is, righteousness; that is, sin and evil must pass away therein from before God, *and men become righteous before God and well pleasing to Him.*"

ARTICLE III. *Of judgment because the prince of this world is judged.* The judgment of which Christ here speaks is to be understood, of course, as being effected by himself in the joint agency of the Paraclete, just as, in the other two cases, the reproving of sin and of righteousness are declared to be. And by adding this last article, his syllabus of doctrine or magazine stock of spiritual armory is made up. For when the transgressor is reproved of sin because of his unbelief, and has the righteousness of God revealed to be upon him when believingly accepted, evidently one thing more and only one is needed to cut off delay and determine promptly his decisive choice of salvation; viz., that some stunning blow of judgment be laid on the idols of his world-worship—the fashions, follies, splendors of condition, expectations of wealth and power, that fasten him by their detentive grasp. When these gods of the earth are laid low and stripped of their fascinations, then the Spirit will have every thing at his advantage, and his triumph will be easy and sure.

The judgment of this world.

Christ means exactly this when he says, "The prince of this world is judged." He is recognizing, I conceive, the fact that evil, though in its very nature a disorganizer, is yet a fearfully despotic organizer also; using all the over-captivating shows and fascinations of our temporal state, to build a kingdom in the bad and of the bad; rallying, as by a naturally malign power, all haters of truth and righteousness in a kind of profane concert; applauding and setting in honor modes of false opinion, that have no show of interlock save in their common opposition to God; making standards of fashions that approve and sanction corrupt usages and manners and shows and pleasures, setting them in such eminence of splendor that society itself is taken, and the captives rush in every where to seize the prize that captivates—able never to resist a fashion; gathering in also the state-craft powers, as perhaps the Saviour intimates, when he speaks of "the prince of this world," and giving over into their hand the money-force and the military, and even the religious, to build bulwarks of wicked statesmanship, that may be held as fortifications against liberty and right for whole ages of time. Hence what he is here saying of "the world" and "the prince of this world" as the bad kingdom he is concerned to judge and cast down. His mind had, in fact, been running in this vein during all the years of his previous ministry. As we see at a very early time, when he sent out the seventy to preach and do mighty works, and when some of them reported on return, saying, "Even the devils are subject unto us through thy name;" and he thereupon broke out in a sharply ecstatic exclamation, as he was almost never known to do before in his very sober style of ministration—"I beheld Satan as lightning fall from heaven." He does not speak indicatively thus, as if he saw the actual precipitation, but prophetically, or proleptically, even as he does here when he says—"Now is the judgment of this world, now is the prince of this world cast out." And he means by the casting out also what he says again shortly after—"The prince of this world cometh and hath nothing in me." And this again is just what he intends by the being judged, for it is the manner of judgment to cast out, or separate, as being in no terms of character that permit communication. "Depart" is the sentence, and "hath nothing in me" is the same. Not that Christ proposes here to separate or be separated from the world. It is no matter of final judgment that concerns him now. He is going rather by the very death scene now at hand, to draw all men unto him. He only means that there is a kind of judgment-day before the judgment, now to be passed, in which he will let his divine attitude and action over opposite the world be distinctly seen, and the despotic rage and madness of the world be visibly humbled and convicted of weakness. The real judgment after death is, of course, a different matter. In these dreadful hours preceding the cross, we are to see the bad empire totter; in that future judgment we are to see it prostrate and forever blasted.

One very important conclusion will, I think, be impressed by a revision of the scene; viz., that the principal actors and spectators have *The actors lose* their courage taken away, and con- *courage.* sciously feel that they are judged, subsiding into a level of dejection that has nothing in common with the very great character on whom their enmity is wreaked. It follows too as a matter of course that the impressions we trace in them, also become ours by the immediate sense of our fallen nature itself. Indeed it might even have been worth the cost, for Christ to go through these horrible scenes of abuse and bitter passion, if it had only been to show evil in its place, and bring down the pompous inanities of sin to the underling state of weakness which is their true significance.

Plainly enough Judas and Peter are both put under judgment, one to die by his own self-avenging instinct, the other to be dreadfully pierced and broken by his Master's judgment glance. Annas and Caiaphas hate Christ fiercely enough to be strong against him, had they not cunning and hypocrisy enough in them to be made ingeniously weak instead. They are full of expedients, and especially the latter, who a few days before, when the council was called on the raising of Lazarus, had his plan to put every thing right; and so confident was he in it, that he could say—" Ye know nothing at all, nor consider that it is expedient that one man should die for the people, and not that the whole nation perish." The true wisdom is, do you not see it? to kill the man, and not have the whole nation itself killed by him, or blotted out on his account by the Romans. So they voted, and from that day forth had it for their counsel. And now he is in hand as their prisoner, the prisoner specially of Caiaphas, and we are to see what the man of high expedients will do with him. Which will be just nothing but the raising of a very contemptible scene of bluster, designed to intimidate Christ and provoke a storm of popular fury against him. In this all the great policies and expediencies appear to be quite used up. But the night coming on will give time to consider what next, and in particular to consider whether a little

Judas and Peter and the high priests.

caution may not also be expedient? And then behold, in the morning it is concluded that as the crime of Jesus has been religious, they had best turn the question over to the civil power; for if Christ should break out as Messiah in a grand religious uprising, that kind of reaction might be dangerous for them. On the whole it is very modestly agreed that the case must go to Pilate.

Very early, therefore, in the morning, Caiaphas and his attendants are before the door of Pilate's judgment hall with the prisoner; where a very pious scruple takes him, and he can not go in lest he be defiled, and so disqualified for the passover! But Pilate very graciously comes out and makes a beginning in the porch, asking—"What accusation bring ye against this man?" And Caiaphas answers tamely enough, letting cautiously down the storm he so tragically raised against yesterday's blasphemy—"If he were not a malefactor we would not have brought him unto thee." And then most deferentially Pilate answers—"Take ye him and judge him according to your law." Whereupon the man of great expediencies rejoins—"It is not lawful for us to put any man to death." And this is the last of what he is able to do, save that afterwards, when it is quite safe, we find him out among the multitude crying, "Crucify him." He has been rushing forward in great purpose, and drawing backward in great caution, and doubling and dodging till the state of nimble confusion is

Pilate judged.

proved to be the utmost result he can accomplish.

At this point we leave him and turn ourselves to the trial as carried on by the Roman magistrate himself. Pilate is a gentleman; a procurator of the Roman Empire, thoroughly versed in its usages and laws, and a man of personal culture generally, though very little of a Puritan, as regards the moral significance of his proceedings. Representing in his own person the general empire, he becomes almost officially the Prince of this World. And we shall shortly see that, as such, he is being judged himself, and utterly broken down. With all his plausible airs, he has yet no sense of justice. He will acquit his prisoner again and again, and will forthwith order him scourged to please his enemies, or deliver him over to them to be insulted and abused, as they may best like. He wants to please every body—to justify the accused because he deserves it—to gratify the priests because they are a great power in the state—to approve himself to Cæsar because he has his office from Cæsar—to win the applause of the multitude because their favor is the necessary condition of successful magistracy. So that just as all sin is confounded by trying to grasp impossible and contrary objects, he falls out of counsel, and is pitched about hither and thither, as if the idea of justice were lost and could not be found.

He carries on the questioning with a certain air of good nature and respectfulness, for the strange man before him shows a majesty and weight of character not to be disregarded. And Christ is the more deferential to him for that reason, which makes the answers he gives all the more impressive. "Art thou the King of the Jews?" With marvelous dignity and a nobly balanced moderation he replies—"Sayest thou this of thyself, or did others tell it thee of me?" Is it proposed to try me thus on the loose talk of the town, or on what you know concerning me? However, I am a king, avowing it with no offense; for my kingdom is not of this world. My kingdom is truth, and "every one that is of the truth heareth my voice." Pilate is dashed and confounded, for he never heard of truth before in this all-worlds' sense of religion, and he rejoins on the instant—What is truth? So deeply impressed is he by the mysterious something of the words and the man, that he waits no answer, but sallies forth to give his acquittal.

But the multitude, who are holding court outside, are dissatisfied, and vent their impatience in loud cries. Whereupon Pilate, who is bound to please the people, gives up Jesus to be scourged, and dressed in mock symbols of royalty, and finally, since they will not cease crying, "crucify him! crucify him!" he gives consent and says, "Take ye him and crucify him; for I find no fault in him." What a *for* is that on which to hang a sentence of death! Crucify him, for there is no justice in it! But it comes to Pilate's ear, by the accusing talk of the Jews, that the prisoner had made himself the Son of God. Very un-Roman language certainly, and what if his wonderful dignity should be somehow connected with a truth so high, in a relationship so divine. When Pilate therefore heard that saying he was the more afraid—so much afraid that he begins to think of a reconsideration, and at once resumes the questioning. Christ at first refuses to answer; for why should he consent to answer in a trial that means nothing, and can not stand by its own verdict? Pilate does not put him under guard, and compel him to answer, but he uses words more urgent—" Knowest thou not that I have power to crucify thee, and power to release thee?" The answer is moderately toned, but is all the more impressive, that there is a sense of silent thunder in it—" Thou couldest have no power at all against me, except it were given thee from above; therefore he that delivered me unto thee hath the greater sin." All at once Pilate feels as if the atmosphere of the court were growing sacred, or as if he had Apollo or Jupiter before him. And just here it was, if I rightly judge, that his wife's note came to hand telling him, " Have thou nothing to do with that just man, for the gods have set me dreaming ill because of him." What then shall he do? for not even the Roman Empire in him dares proceed. He can go no farther, for he has, in fact, no magistracy left. He can only wash his hands to be clear of the innocent blood, and throw it over on the poor weak multitude, to take the responsibility he is himself in no resolution to bear, and to say, "his blood be upon us and upon our children."

Now it may be that some of us are grown so familiar with this story of Pilate, that we shall not sufficiently apprehend the judgment- *Pilate makes court to Herod.* day look of it. If it be so, there is yet one fact that will give us a very truly convincing test of it. Pilate, and Herod, the provincial magistrate of Galilee, had hitherto been enemies, on terms of personal non-intercourse. But Pilate now takes advantage of the presence of Herod in the city, and sends over Christ to Herod's quarters, to be examined by him. And the result is, we are told, that from that day they were made friends together. Here then we have a man of dignity, a man who well understands what belongs to public character and the highest statesmanship, who is put on being reconciled to his enemy, by what? Why by what he apprehends from a poor tradesman, a simple, inoffensive, inaggressive person, who is set before him only to be his victim—a man without power, showing no resentments, offering not a sign of resistance. And to make sure against him, he undertakes to strengthen himself by joining hands with his great public enemy! No, there is more in the case than what I have given by this mere external description. In this man Christ there is visibly some untried talent or resource. Such have not frequently appeared either in Jerusalem or at Rome. There is an appalling moral force in his bearing, should we not rather say, a conspicuously divine force? He somehow stirs the superstition of Pilate's nature. For outwardly composed as he is, and as the pride of character requires, he is yet anxious inwardly, and even disconcerted. He can not guess what great upturning, or public revolution, may be coming to pass, by the agency of this certainly most remarkable character. Some wondrous future must be wrapped up in his person. His look contains a mystery, his words are set like oracles. Call it talent, command, authority of soul, something there is in him that makes every thing seem possible. Probably Pilate does not run out his thought in just these forms, but he quails inwardly in his feeling, in a way that comprehends the sense of these indications. Without knowing it, he is at a point of concern that really unmans him, and by this kind of instigation, which he is not quite aware of himself, he is put on conciliating Herod by these extraordinary advances.

Omitting farther reference now to the conduct of the particular and more forward parties in the trial, the aspect of judgment, we shall see, covers the whole transaction. Including every thing done by the priests, and the soldiers, and the multitude, it bears a character of low brutality and basely exasperated passion, that we can nowise account for, considering the beautiful inoffensiveness and silent worth of the victim; save in the supposition of some judicial madness that for the time has demonized so many people. And we do this with the

<small>The judgment looks general.</small>

better reason that a correspondently disturbed behavior shakes the frame and darkens the face of nature itself. The rocks themselves are shuddering in the agitation, and the blackened sun can not look on the sight! And what is the feeling coming on us all, but exactly that which fell on all the actors and beholders concerned, when the hour of sanity and right understanding arrived—"And all the people that came together to that sight, beholding the things that were done, smote their breasts and returned!" They had seen the prince of this world judged, and had felt the judgment also in themselves. They smote their breasts, for the bad kingdom there had received a stunning blow. Calling it the crucifixion-day for one party, it is yet more conspicuously a scene by which the other is judged and cast down. From that day to this the prince of this world has had a reduced and broken look. Men of Christian countries are visited in evil with a special kind of misgiving; for they have seen, in the dreadful story of Christ's trial scene, how weak is the pride and the force-principle too of this world, when it is put in issue with simple character—how it comes out as a culprit judged, even after its rage is spent, and after it has had its own way to the fatal end.

And here at last comes up into view the great fact which underlies this whole matter of the reproving of judgment; viz., that mere divine force could not compass it, *No judgment by force, but only by goodness.* and that nothing but the majesty of moral suffering could. Since God is omnipotent, many are ready, in foolish haste, to imagine that he can therefore bring in upon evil and the prince of this world, what reproving of judgment he will. Doubtless he can make a judgment-day in force that will trample down all sin, and be an everlasting extirpation of it. But the probability is that it would trample and extirpate all being as well. What is wanted is a casting down of evil in beings still existing, still to exist. And nothing could do that but some trial scene or crucifixion-day, that allows it to be seen coping with pure excellence or the suffering capacity of goodness without force. Then it is so visibly defeated by victory that it bears a weak and fallen look. The victory is plainly on the other side. Hence the awful prostration brought on all the active parties in the crucifixion-scene when once it was over. And it was to be a reproving of judgment in just this way, and to continue to be even to the end of the world. There was, in short, no other way of breaking down the prince of this world and the pride of evil bodied in his kingdom, but to let the eternal patience meet him as it well knows how. For this purpose too, in great part, Christ was incarnate. For "as the children are partakers of flesh and blood, he also himself likewise took part of the same; that through death he might destroy him that had the power of death, that is the devil."* This word death, as I conceive, is to be taken in its largest sense; viz., that only death could

---

* Heb. ii, 14.

slay the killer—that the bad power could be nowise broken by force, but that it must needs be done by suffering, whereby it is proved to be weak, cast down, reproved of judgment. We have still another passage of Scripture that has had much difficulty in finding its meaning. "For what the law could not do, in that it was weak through the flesh, God sending his own Son in the likeness of sinful flesh, and for sin, condemned sin in the flesh, that the righteousness of the law might be fulfilled in us, who walk not after the flesh but after the Spirit."* Here again we have the argument turned upon the fact of an incarnation; and the result, viz., a bringing out into spirit and righteous liberty, hinges on a condemnation, that is on a *judgment* of sin; for the word means *adverse judgment*, and is the same that we have been handling in these illustrations. Coming *for* sin, Christ must needs condemn sin, or bring down a reproving of judgment on it that will loosen its grasp. For the grinding it to powder, even as Moses ground the golden calf, would not take it away. No force could accomplish the dislodgment. It must be worsted and judged by suffering character. In that lies the victory and dear great mystery of the cross.

Having made our exposition thus of Christ's threefold doctrine as related to the reproving of sin, of righteousness, and of judgment, it may be required of us to state more explicitly

<small>What we mean.</small>

---

* Romans viii. 3, 4.

how much or how little we mean by it, and what are to be the uses served by it.

It was evidently not the Saviour's intention to draw out what was afterwards called by theologians a syllabus of doctrine. It does not appear that any such notion had as yet dawned on the mind of any disciple, or teacher. Dogmatic statements, or formulated propositions of doctrine, were to make their appearance farther on, and perhaps to have a certain legitimate use, but they very plainly had not yet arrived. The Saviour had none but a practical meaning in his threefold specification; viz., to so inaugurate the Spirit, as to give a properly intelligent conception of his outfit, as the BRINGER-IN for salvation. He was to be a kind of invisible preacher present with the preachers, taking the things of Christ, and weaving them into the new experience of men. And the result was to be that, from and after his death, all that he had been doing by his personal ministry was to be a dispensation-force, in this manner, of life and truth for all the coming ages. According to his own conception it will be sufficient and complete, and will so be called, as afterwards by Paul, "the ministration of the Spirit."

This threefold specification of the Saviour is a doctrine extra, that it will be most agreeable to recur to
<small>No rival doctrine meant.</small> and hold, because it is given by Christ himself. I only conceive that in giving it I give another, more intensely practical doctrine,

outlined for us by Christ, which may be used, with great advantage, as a complementary mode of teaching and statement, and will not work derangement or hurtful disorder if it should sometimes be allowed, where the mind is late in coming into satisfaction by the other forms, to dominate, or determine the methods of preaching. It certainly can not be imagined that preaching what Christ himself gave to be the outfit of the Holy Spirit, in his saving ministration, is not preaching Christ. Besides there is such an agreement, or accord, between the more theologic forms of doctrine, built up round the terms of law and sacrifice, and this which I am here proposing to add as another and different, that, partly by reason of their difference, they will be always asking for each other. It will be as if the former were coming over to this to find the regulative mode of preaching, and this latter going back to the other to find the basal ideas at which the grace begins. And it should not be an offense to add, that the very thing most wanted now, in this great subject, is the conceded right and familiar use of other forms of doctrine differently conceived, and yet in virtual agreement. By long ages of use and speculative reiteration we have been running down all the scripture figures of propitiation, sacrifice, atonement, imputed righteousness, and the like, into stunted literalities, till the words themselves have become, in fact, lost words, and can by no advertising be recovered. We shall never get them back, till we relax the rigors of literality by letting in other forms, to have an accordant authority and use. We shall thus and then begin to recover the living ideas we had killed, by the dry-timber words, in which we put them, and finally to recover the living and flexible senses of the words themselves. The speculating, over-dogmatizing habit that has been pressing us into the literal method, has also, for the same reason, been making our gospel narrow and close, and a more nearly choking bondage than either it could afford to be, or we to make it. And thus again, for a double reason, we are to have our account in almost any variety of gospel version, that will take us clear of the nearly fatal syncope of our literal tethers, and give us a more easy play in the figures and poetic liberties of the truth.

Thus Christ, in his first article of doctrine, says, "Of sin because they believe not on me," expecting evidently that by his cross of sacrifice, a new sense of sin will be wakened in the newly wakened sensibilities of his rejectors, and in that fact discovers, in great part certainly, the value of his sacrifice. But we have a speculated form of belief which has gotten clear of the figurative meaning of sacrifice, maintaining that Christ is a literal sacrifice, which, being offered for our sin, evens up our account with God, and yields us a remission that is in fact complete immunity.

How the letter palls.

So in his reproving of righteousness, Christ conceives himself to be the righteousness of God charactered in outward figure, in his human life, whereupon the guilty world coming to him by faith, are to have it in them by assimilation, or a certain divine contagion, having it not from themselves, but only as being acted consentingly into it. Thus much in the free, figure-painting way; over against which we have had it long made up in quantitative, almost arithmetic terms, that Christ has suffered pains enough for us, to pay the whole debt of the law, and so far has become a righteousness for us; not a righteousness that makes us righteous at all, but that only evens the books. To name all the misconceptions by which we have robbed the free scripture of its meaning in this manner, is impossible. We shall never get back the ideas lost, till we allow the possibility of double, and treble, and quadruple forms. And for one of these, I can think of nothing better and more reverent to suggest, than that which Christ himself has here propounded.

Now it will be imagined, not unlikely by some, that there is a want of scope in this threefold version of the Saviour, which forbids its being used in any sense for a summation of doctrine. And to this I answer that it is not wanted for a summation of doctrine. We have had enough of that. What we want a great deal more is something to give us greater breadth of standing and greater vitality of idea. And yet some will imagine that when Christ announces, first, the reproving of sin, and then the reproving of righteousness, he only gives us to say, as we have so long been saying, till

Full scope in the three articles.

we have worn out the meaning of the routine words themselves—first conviction, then conversion; first the law, and then the Spirit; whereas there is scarcely a hair's weight in common between this representation and that which Christ is giving. The proposed conviction of sin is not here by the law, or by any computation of sins and deserved penalties, but it is to be by the gospel rather, and to come, not as being bolted in by the legal majesty of Sinai, but as being melted in by the suffering goodness of Christ. It is to be a new and tender sensibility to sin, raised in the soul, by what Christ has done for it, and above all by what it has hitherto refused to let him do for it. The chapter he has made for it is heavy with sorrow. It is infinite love tracking its approach in tears and blood. And the story is so deep, and full, and various, and tender, raises so many questions, opens so many vistas into the divine nature and life, and so many others down the guilty slopes of humanity within, that the whole nature both of God and man are seen to be stirred in mutuality together.

It is plainly to be seen that Christ, in his reproving of righteousness, has no reference to the hard-favored scheme of legal justification commonly held. By the "reproving" he means, I suppose, the new apprehension, or new sensibility to righteousness, that will be quickened by the revelation of it made in his person, and that, after he has gone up to the Father to be seen here no more, it will be upon the world as a power of holy remembrance, and a new possibility of character. He has not come out from God to pay up our penal debts, but to raise an impression for character. And the righteousness he brings is all for all, free as the day and large as free—a grace that undertakes to fill no petty computations of bad liability, but simply floods and overflows the utmost receptivity it finds.

Let it also be noted that Christ does not mean by his "reproving of judgment" the same thing over again which he has declared in his "reproving of sin." It is not his way to squander words on loose repetitions. I have undertaken also to show that his reproving of judgment is a wholly different matter, raising initial constructions that may be carried farther and probably with great advantage. Last named by Christ in his threefold doctrine, we seem to see that he rates the consequence of this article highest. And yet it has somehow gotten hold of theologic ideas but slowly. By how many is it preached, by how many is it distinctly conceived. Have we not some right to suspect, that the very thing most wanted now is a due impression of the tyranny of the prince of this world and of the judgment-force Christ has set against the bad kingdom to bring it down. Is there not possibly a preaching of Christ that should have the same effects, in all ages and communities, that were wrought by the scene of the Cross.

On the whole I can not admit that any theologian, or church, or council, has ever drawn a larger base of doctrine, or more rich, than Christ himself has given us in his threefold stock of gospel outfit. Here, in fact, is the whole Christian System, without any pretense of system; and the doctrine of the Spirit given by Christ himself.

SUPPLEMENTARY NOTES.

SUPPLEMENTARY NOTES.

In these notes I propose no controversy, but only to use the suggestive helps my critics give me in preparing a more specific and sufficient statement.

NOTE 1, p. 39.

Thus it has been objected, *in limine*, that the difficulties we ourselves encounter in the matter of our human forgivenesses are caused by the moral obliquity of our state of sin; but God, having no such corruption of nature, wants, of course, no such mitigation or propitiation of his feeling in order to the forgiveness of his enemies; and is, therefore, in no terms of analogy with us. But there is a manifest oversight in the objection. We commonly take it for granted, I admit, that the reluctations we encounter in preaching forgiveness are simply wicked, and that overcoming the virulences of the bad mind is, in such cases, the whole matter. We do not observe that a considerable part of their tenacity, and the part that is slowest often to yield, is due to causes that are innocent—viz., to the just indignations raised in our moral nature itself by the injuries to be forgiven. These indignations come by their own law, and give us no option. But we very greatly mistake, when we make this natural tenacity an integral part of the wicked obstinacy encountered in preaching forgiveness, or trying to practice the forgiving temper. The obstinacy, so-called, is blamable only so far as it is created by selfish passion aggravating the offence, by wounded pride and grudging resentments. So far, it is a fit subject of repentance; for the rest, it is even justifiable, and will most easily be overcome by so regarding it; with the conviction added that it is best and most certainly removed, as God's indignations are, by a patient endurance of the adversary, and by making cost for his benefit; *i.e.*, by propitiation. In a different way of treatment, making all the difficulties in forgiveness chargeable with blame, we put it on men to stifle their nature instead of their sin, in which, of course, they will have just that doubtful success which we are so often obliged to deplore.

Besides, the just indignations of our moral nature require to be stiffly asserted, and not too easily remitted. They are the natural vindicators of law, supplying the severities that are its necessary arguments. Moreover, they belong to the eternal reason of character; for if there be forgiveness, whether in God or man, it should come gradually, and by a measured and modulated sorrow that steadies the moral attitude and takes away all appearance of laxity. No being can have character who is simply spilling his forgivenesses without any fit assertion of his indignations, or care what becomes of his wrongs. Having a moral nature, it is not for him to just let his indignations die and be taken out of the way, as if they had no reason why they should exist. There was a reason, and it must be somehow fulfilled. To let all these condemnations and wrath-fires of the moral system fall through into nothingness, would reduce it to a very absurd figure. God has not so cast the plan of it, but he will bring it through by a different method: viz., by making cost for the transgressors and letting his sorrow-burdened love melt away his indignations. Herein we are to behold the transcendent majesty of his imperial patience. In this way there is no offensive rigor left, and his divine authority is exalted by just that which the forgiveness yields of great expression.

NOTE 2, pp. 59–63.

The relation of analogy, in which I have set the propitiation by Christ, and the propitiations by which we, as men, bring ourselves into a real and true forgiveness of our fellow men, has incurred the blame of some, as being a virtual desecration of the subject. Are we thus to represent that God, the All Perfect, is obliged to fight his way back into forgiveness, through repugnances, revulsions, and disgusts of bad remembrance, and savors of old offence, even as we are? But the savors of such remembrance and offence he certainly has; for, having a moral nature, the wrongs of transgression have all been violations of his righteous sensibility. So far, he is in exactly our condition as regards the offences of wrong; and what shall he do to recompose the state of peace with his adversaries? If he should receive the penalties they have incurred, from a suffering substitute, that would be no satisfaction to the offence of his feeling, which is truly wounded feeling as before.

And what do we better know as men, at our poor distracted level of character, than that wrongs to our personal feeling are never to be redressed by pay, or by the enactions of revenge, or even by the visible judgments of Providence; or, in fact, by anything but simply bearing them in voluntary cost and sweet-minded endurance, issued in free forgiveness? And what if we should add, so it is with God? What we find in the small, in our own moral nature, we venture also to look for in the nobler nature of God as our Eternal Father. Only it is our misfortune that we have to invert the natural order, discovering what is true of God from what is true of ourselves, when, if putting our argument in the order of nature, we had only to show our need of propitiation from a like need in him, there would be no look of offence.

We also reduce, or seem to reduce, the pitch of his dignity in the statement of this analogy, by reason of the necessary infirmity of language. Language beholds everything in time, or as taking place in the tense of grammar; and there is no tense for God that begins at his eternity. He is representable, therefore, only in time with ourselves and our activities. So that when we put him in analogy with ourselves, in the struggles and revulsions by which we come into forgiveness, we behold him dragging himself heavily in by a transactional process, and, as we may say, getting himself under to forgive. Whereas, our only way to behold him in his dignity, is to conceive him as complete in all his dispositions, before his transactions begin. There was a New Testament in him thus, before the historic Old, written out in cipher as the world-story planned for, to be suffered in, magnified by, embalmed in, forgivenesses already ripe. Christ, when he comes, does not so much create this gospel as bring us the key, and show us the transactional form, under laws of tense in the grammar of our human speech. As being historical, it is an accommodation thus to our modes of thought and knowledge; and has put upon it, in this way, a certain undivine *ex post facto* look, as if God were coming along *after* sins, to recompose his feeling and keep himself in a forgiving temper. Whereas, if we rightly conceive him, he has been in this work as in counsel, and moving through it in feeling from eternity. He knew the liberty there was to be in his creature and all that would come of it—the sin to be rooted in the liberty, and the suffering and wrong to be rooted in both; every sorrow to be waited for, pitied, supported; all the offences, stings of sensibility, scorches of wrath; the disgusts, loathings, commiserations of wickedness;—a vast ante-mundane thought-picture that was ever before him, and was only not the cross, because it was a sacrifice transacted within, so much greater than it could be without, so much greater in the overspread of his eternity than it could be in the bleeding of a day. And yet, in some most worthy and sacred sense, one is the other, and both are in the type or fixed analogy of our own small cost, endured when we pass a clean forgiveness of our enemy. In this analogy thoughtfully viewed, God is nowise diminished, but transcendently magnified, rather.

But the discussion we are in, at this point, is not fairly ended, till we take in a different matter that lies outside of these debates of analogy; viz., that a real propitiation, such as I am trying here to assert, requires a radically different God, higher in quality and more genially sovereign—one who rules in passibility of sentiment, and tempers order and counsel by infusions of tragic life. The God of a supra-lapsarian theology, doing everything by will and nothing by sentiment, may have the word propitiation set in his articles; but he is scarcely more capable of the meaning than impassive rock. He cannot be wounded or crossed; and if we speak of his pity, his relentings, his loathings, his afflictions for the good, his abhorrence of the wicked, and all the various pains of his sensibility, we only consider it, and probably call it, our speaking after the manner of men. In all this, there is no thought that something has taken place that is really counter to the will of God; but sin exists only because it is wanted, and he is the author of it. Crimes occur against order and law, simply because he will have them violated. Repentance takes place just so far as he is concerned to have it. Christ dies for all, but with no care to save any but the elect. He suffers only in his human part; for the rock of Calvary is not more impassive to suffering than his divine nature. How then, having such a God, is there going to be any mitigation, or assuagement, or pacified wrath, that can be called propitiation? A change is permitted in the treatment of transgressors it is claimed, because Christ has borne the penalties of the law, and paid in legal satisfaction; but no sentiment of God is at all differently moved or affected. All there is of motion or emotion to make greatness of character is just where it was, and his excellence is summed up in his completely infrangible sufficiency. No ultimation is ever coming forth or to come, that displays the magnanimity of his injured feeling, or any passive virtue, or any softer motivity than absolute will. He is a God to be magnified in no endurances, for he has them not.

Let it now be assumed, going back to the time when God has all things in possibility, and nothing as yet created, that in moving the plan of a creation, he meets the question occurrent, whether it shall be stocked with creatures morally related to himself, or such as are not so related, such as have no sense of right and wrong, and no religious aspiration reaching after society with himself? A world of creatures unrelated thus to himself will be more easily managed, because they have no endowment of liberty. He puts them in law himself, and they will go by their law with no possibility of question. They can be made happy as birds, filling the air with notes of glad feeling that are only not hymns. They may be set upon their feet to walk the earth erect in stately forms, composing a joyous herdship in the finest amiabilities of instinct, and only not society. Under no moral obligation, they are subject to no moral catastrophe. And yet, when we speak of them as creatures morally unrelated to God, we can see at a glance, I think, that God will require a different population. Doubtless he will want creatures personally related or morally akin to himself, such as can receive his dispositions, enter into his thoughts, and have some due valuation of what is highest in his character. He can be their Eternal Father to such, when he could not to the others any more than to the cattle in the fields.

But there is a terrible alternative connected; they must

be creatures in liberty, having in that fearful endowment, a like fearful possibility, or rather certainty, of breaking out of law, and being precipitated into misrule and corruption. Aspiring to be gods, they will fill the world with havoc and disorder. Wars and deeds of blood will be another name for human affairs. The power of liberty will turn out thus to be a woe-birth power of lust and vice and heavy loathsomeness. Can it be that God will prefer a world in these bad liabilities? It is easy to conclude that he will, because he has done it. This, no doubt, for the reason that he can bring more character out of it, and higher and more akin to his own, more love and majesty and worth and real greatness.

But in that creative counsel and choice, how much does he consent to endure. The terrible tragedies of wrong are all let loose. His empire is an ocean wild with storm. His creatures morally related to himself become so many patiences demanded. They dare even blasphemy against him, and, what is worse to his feeling, they dare to be loathsome and miserable. What he means to have society, they dare to dissolve by terror, rapine, and lust. And all these woes stand related to his feeling, as woes in morally related beings inevitably must. His fatherly nature is moved in abhorrences and sorrows, and in throes of tragic life. And what is the conclusion brought us but that, as the whole world-story is a transaction of cost to his divine feeling, he will be propitiated already, before the time, for every one that wants to be forgiven for his sins. Every transgressor has been with him and before him even from eternity, suffered for with even a bleeding patience. And does any one imagine that a God who has been bearing all the storms and heavy woes of his bad populations for so many ages, bearing every particular transgressor with a particular concern, cannot, when the time arrives, find how to forgive him? God has been atoning him, as we speak, all the way down his eternity, by what he has been suffering for him,—is he still unready to forgive him? True, the propitiation thus conceived is of a date long prior to the trangression, and one that has been going on for eternal ages. All the more ready and profoundly sure will the forgiveness be.

We can never understand the depth and reality of God's propitiations till we behold him in the counsel of creation, taking up his burden of cost, and carrying it on down the tragic ages with him, in a line of patience that dates from the beginning. In Christ and the cross, he is representatively ready, and many of us think he is made ready after that date; but all such as are able to think him worthily, understand that he was not less ready before, but is now in Christ more sufficiently declared to be.

NOTE 3, p. 120.

It happens that these two words *law* and *commandment* are used together with a like close relationship of meaning, in a whole series of verses in the 7th Chapter of the Epistle to the Romans. I will not undertake to say that they are used in the sense of my present exposition. I certainly do not think they have ever been so interpreted. The commentators never undertake to show how they occur thus together, or in what manner they were brought in to be elements together in such a discussion. They commonly end off at once their account of the word "Commandment," by simply saying that it means a specific injunction of what is more generally contained in the total authority of the law. But they do not stop to observe the very palpable unfitness of the word, thus clumsily defined, to serve any one of the uses put upon it. For example, when the apostle says: "I was alive without the law once, but when the commandment came, sin revived, and I died," how could he be without the law, and have the commandment come as being a specific injunction drawn out of the law? And what is it for the commandment to come, when there is no law at hand to enjoin it? Whence in such a case does it come? Who speaks it? Out of what height or depth or silence?

If we go back to the 6th verse, we find two ideas occurring conjunctively, which are staple in my exposition, viz., "letter and spirit," ideas congenially related to law and commandment, and it may be that such ideas concurrent bring on the general argument in which they stand. At any rate, Paul has the two words in hand together, whether we can find how he came to set them balancing and working in such manner or not; and he will use them according to, and not against, their nature. And as spirit is, in its very nature, but another name for the liberty of Christ, it does not seem incredible that he is using the commandment in the sense of spirit and liberty, much as I have here been doing. Nor is it any objection to this, that it supposes a killing power in the commandment as well as in the law, for this exactly is the work of Christ until he is embraced by faith—"of sin, because they believe not on me." Nor does this at all hinder the apostle's boast of deliverance—"I thank God, through Jesus Christ our Lord;" for the coming in of Christ as the life, is always found to be unto death: until he is practically embraced in his justifying power.

How far off then these two words *law* and *commandment*, as used by the apostle, are from the more particular construction I have given them, in the statement of their relative uses and meanings, I will not undertake to judge. There may be one or many shades of difference, with quite as good a chance of one or many shades of coincidence. And this should be the less remarkable, that the commentators, in all their huge wrestlings over the chapter, do not appear to have had any really close questioning about the two words

—what they are here for, and how they came, and what they are doing with the argument.

NOTE 4, p. 208.

Since the publication of my revised interpretation, I have fallen upon a statement of justification—quoted by Michelet in his Life of Luther (pp. 12, 13.),—which differs widely as possible from the impression I had received of his doctrine, and not less widely, I think, from the general impression of his adherents and followers. The language of his statement is the more remarkable, that it was uttered only one or two years before his death, at which time, speculative language would be apt to lose its ascendency, and practical to take its place. He plainly enough means, by justice, that regenerative righteousness by which God is revealed in character, —the righteousness of God by faith.

" Even when I was at school, in studying the Epistles of St. Paul, I was seized with the most ardent desire to understand what the apostle meant in his Epistle to the Romans. One single phrase stopped me: *Justitia Dei revelatur in illo.* I hated this expression, *Justitia Dei*, because, according to the custom of doctors, I had learned to understand by it that active justice, whereby God is just, and punishes the unjust and sinners. Now, I, who led the life of a harmless monk, and who yet felt painfully within me the uneasy conscience of a sinner, without being able to attain an idea as to the satisfaction I might offer up to God, I did not love, nay, to say the truth, I hated this just God, punisher of sin. I was indignant against Him, and gave silent utterance to murmuring, if not altogether to blasphemy. I said to myself: ' Is it not, then, enough that wretched sinners, already eternally damned for original sin, should be overwhelmed with so many calamities by the decrees of the decalogue, but God must further add misery to misery by his gospel, menacing us even there with his justice and his anger?' It was thus the trouble of my conscience carried me away, and I always came back to the same passage. At last, I perceived that the *justice* of God is that whereby, with the blessing of God, the just man lives, that is to say, *Faith;* and I then saw that the meaning of the passage was thus: *The gospel reveals the justice of God, a passive justice, whereby the merciful God justifies us by faith.* Thereupon, I felt as if born again, and it seemed to me as though heaven's gates stood full open before me, and that I was joyfully entering therein. At a later period, I read St. Augustine's book, *On the Spirit and the Letter,* and I found, contrary to my expectations, that he also understands by the justice of God, that wherewith God clothes us in justifying us. I was greatly rejoiced to find this, though the thing is put somewhat incompletely in the book, and though the father explains hinself vaguely and imperfectly, on the doctrine of imputation."

In this life of Luther, is cited at large, also, the dialogue that passed between himself and Melancthon, on justification by faith, taking exactly the ground that I have taken, making justification a continuous grace, and not a grace gone by, and cut short by the preterite verb that describes it. (p. 427).

Melancthon: When you say: We are justified only by faith, do you understand that only from the beginning of the remission of sins?

Luther: From the beginning, from the middle, and from the end. * * * No piecing or partial cause approaches thereunto; for faith is powerful continually without ceasing; otherwise, it is no faith. Therefore of what value the works are, the same they are through the honor and power of faith, which undeniably is the sun or sun-beam of this shining.

, Catalogues of the publications of SCRIBNER, ARMSTRONG & CO and of the importations of SCRIBNER, WELFORD & ARMSTRONG will be sent to any address upon application.

Standard Text-Books
AND
Works of Reference,
PUBLISHED BY
SCRIBNER, ARMSTRONG & CO.,
743 and 745 Broadway, New York.

N.B.—S., A. & Co. will send their Publications by Mail to any part of the U. S., prepaid, on receipt of price.

ART.
	RETAIL PRICES.
TORREY'S THEORY OF FINE ART	$1 50

COMPOSITION.
DAY'S ART OF ENGLISH COMPOSITION	1 50
DAY'S YOUNG COMPOSER	1 00
HARPER'S PRACTICAL COMPOSITION	90

CHEMISTRY.
COOLEY'S TEXT-BOOK OF CHEMISTRY	1 25
COOLEY'S ELEMENTS OF CHEMISTRY	1 00

ECCLESIASTICAL HISTORY.
ALEXANDER'S NOTES ON NEW TESTAMENT LITERATURE AND ECCLESIASTICAL HISTORY	2 00
FISHER'S HISTORY OF THE REFORMATION	3 00
FISHER'S SUPERNATURAL ORIGIN OF CHRISTIANITY	3 00
HAGENBACH'S HISTORY OF THE CHURCH IN THE EIGHTEENTH AND NINETEENTH CENTURIES. 2 vols	6 00
SCHAFF'S HISTORY OF THE APOSTOLIC CHURCH, with a general introduction to Church History	3 75
SCHAFF'S HISTORY OF THE CHRISTIAN CHURCH. 2 vols	7 50
SHEDD'S HISTORY OF THE CHRISTIAN DOCTRINE. 2 vols	5 00
SMITH'S HISTORY OF THE CHURCH OF CHRIST IN CHRONOLOGICAL TABLES	6 75
STANLEY'S LECTURES ON THE HISTORY OF EASTERN CHURCH, with an Introduction on the Study of Ecclesiastical History	2 50
STANLEY'S LECTURES ON THE HISTORY OF THE JEWISH CHURCH.	
PART 1.—ABRAHAM TO SAMUEL	2 50
PART 2.—SAMUEL TO THE CAPTIVITY	2 50
PART 3.—FROM THE CAPTIVITY TO THE CHRISTIAN ERA	4 00
STANLEY'S LECTURES ON THE HISTORY OF THE SCOTTISH CHURCH	2 50

ENGLISH LANGUAGE AND LITERATURE.

RETAIL PRICES.

CLARK'S ELEMENTS OF THE ENGLISH LANGUAGE	$1 25
CRAIK'S HISTORY OF ENGLISH LITERATURE AND LANGUAGE. 2 vols.	5 00
DAY'S INTRODUCTION TO THE STUDY OF ENGLISH LITERATURE.	2 25
DE VERE'S STUDIES IN ENGLISH	2 50
MARSH'S LECTURES ON THE ENGLISH LANGUAGE	3 00
MARSH'S ORIGIN AND HISTORY OF THE ENGLISH LANGUAGE	3 00

FINANCE.

BAGEHOT'S LOMBARD STREET, a Description of the Money Market	1 75
GIBBON'S THE PUBLIC DEBT OF THE UNITED STATES	2 00

HISTORY.

EPOCHS OF HISTORY. A series of concise and carefully prepared works on particular eras of History. Each volume complete in itself. Price per volume............ 1 00

NOW READY.

EPOCHS OF MODERN HISTORY.

—— THE ERA OF THE PROTESTANT RELIGION. By F. SEEBOHM, author of "The Oxford Reformers."
—— THE CRUSADES. By Rev. G. W. Cox, author of "The History of Greece," etc.
—— THE THIRTY YEARS' WAR, 1618–1648. By SAMUEL RAWSON GARDINER.
—— THE HOUSES OF LANCASTER AND YORK, with the Conquest and Loss of France. By JAMES GAIRDNER, Editor of the "Pastor's Letters," etc. With Five Maps.
—— THE FRENCH REVOLUTION AND FIRST EMPIRE: An Historical Sketch. By WILLIAM O'CONNOR MORRIS.
—— THE AGE OF ELIZABETH. By Rev. M. CREIGHTON, M.A.
—— THE FALL OF THE STUARTS; and Western Europe from 1678 to 1697. By Rev. E. HALE, A.M.
—— THE PURITAN REVOLUTION. By S. R. GARDINER, author of "The Thirty Years' War."
—— THE EARLY PLANTAGENETS. By W. STUBBS, M.A., Regius Professor of Modern History in the University of Oxford. With 2 Maps.

Other volumes are in active preparation, and will be duly announced.

EPOCHS OF ANCIENT HISTORY.

—— THE GREEKS AND THE PERSIANS. By the Rev. GEORGE W. COX, M.A., late Scholar of Trinity College, Oxford.
—— THE EARLY EMPIRE. By the Rev. W. WOLFE CAPES, M.A., Reader of Ancient History in the University of Oxford.
—— THE ATHENIAN EMPIRE, from the Flight of Xerxes to the Fall of Athens. By the Rev. G. W. Cox, M.A., Joint Editor of the Series.
—— EARLY ROME. From the foundation of the City to its destruction by the Gauls. By W. IHNE, Ph.D., author of "History of Rome." With a Map.

⁎ To be followed at frequent intervals by the following Works in continuation of the same Series:

—— SPARTAN AND THEBAN SUPREMACY. By CHARLES SANKEY, M.A., late Scholar of Queen's College, Oxford, Joint-Editor of the Series.
—— MACEDONIAN EMPIRE. Its Rise and Culmination to the Death of Alexander the Great. By A. M. CURTEIS, M.A., Assistant-Master, Sherborne School.
—— ROME AND CARTHAGE. THE PUNIC WARS. By R. BOSWORTH SMITH, M.A., Assistant-Master, Harrow School.
—— THE GRACCHI, MARIUS, AND SULLA. By A. H. BEESLY, M.A., Assistant-Master, Marlborough College.

HISTORY.—Continued.

RETAIL PRICES.

——THE ROMAN TRIUMVIRATES. By the Very Rev. CHARLES MERIVALE, D.D., Dean of Ely. (*Shortly*.)
——THE AGE OF TRAJAN AND THE ANTONINES. By the Rev. W. WOLFE CAPES, M.A., Reader of Ancient History in the University of Oxford.

FROUDE'S HISTORY OF ENGLAND, from the FALL of WOOLSEY to the DEATH of ELIZABETH. 12 vols., per set $15 00
FROUDE'S THE ENGLISH IN IRELAND. 3 vols.............................. 7 50
STRICKLAND'S LIVES OF THE QUEENS OF ENGLAND 2 50

HOMILETICS.

ALEXANDER'S THOUGHTS ON PREACHING, being contributions to Homiletics.. 2 00
SHEDD'S TREATISE ON HOMILETICS AND PASTORAL THEOLOGY.. 2 50

HYDRAULICS.

EWBANK'S HYDRAULICS. Ancient and Modern.......................... 6 00

INTERNATIONAL LAW.

WOOLSEY ON INTERNATIONAL LAW, now used as the Government Text-Book at West Point... 2 50

LOGIC.

DAY'S ELEMENTS OF LOGIC... 1 50

MENTAL SCIENCE AND PHILOSOPHY.

HOPKINS' OUTLINE STUDY OF MAN.. 1 75
PLATO'S BEST THOUGHTS.. 2 50
PLATO'S DIALOGUES. Translated by Prof. B. A. JOWETT. 4 vols...... 8 00
PORTER ON THE HUMAN INTELLECT.. 5 00
PORTER'S ELEMENTS OF INTELLECTUAL PHILOSOPHY, being an abridgment of the "Human Intellect".. 3 00
UEBERWEG'S HISTORY OF PHILOSOPHY. 2 vols........................ 5 00

MORAL SCIENCE.

ALEXANDER'S OUTLINES OF MORAL SCIENCE.. .... 1 50
HOPKINS ON THE LAW OF LOVE; or, CHRISTIAN ETHICS.............. 1 75

MYTHOLOGY.

MURRAY'S MANUAL OF MYTHOLOGY... 2 25

NATURAL HISTORY.

AGASSIZ'S THE STRUCTURE OF ANIMAL LIFE............................ 1 50
COOKE'S RELIGION AND CHEMISTRY.. 2 50
SHIELD'S RELIGION AND SCIENCE.. 75

NATURAL PHILOSOPHY.

COOLEY'S TEXT-BOOK OF NATURAL PHILOSOPHY..................... 1 50
COOLEY'S ELEMENTS OF NATURAL PHILOSOPHY 1 00

ORIGIN OF THE BIBLE.

RETAIL PRICES.

ROGERS' SUPERHUMAN ORIGIN OF THE BIBLE, inferred from itself.... $2 00

PHILOLOGY.

DWIGHT'S PHILOLOGY. 2 vols., reduced to............................ 4 00
HALL'S MODERN ENGLISH.. 2 50
HALL'S RECENT EXEMPLIFICATIONS OF FALSE PHILOLOGY........ 1 25
MULLER'S LECTURES ON THE SCIENCE OF LANGUAGE. 2 vols. 6 00
TRENCH'S ENGLISH PAST AND PRESENT................................ 1 25
WHITNEY'S LANGUAGE AND THE STUDY OF LANGUAGE............. 2 50
WHITNEY'S ORIENTAL AND LINGUISTIC STUDIES. Part 1........... 2 50
———— THE SAME. Part 2... 2 50

PHYSICAL GEOGRAPHY.

GUYOT'S THE EARTH AND MAN.. 1 75
MARSH'S THE EARTH AS MODIFIED BY HUMAN ACTION.......... 4 50
MARSH'S MAN AND NATURE.. 3 00

POLITICAL.

DAWSON'S FEDERALIST.. 2 50
SEAMAN'S AMERICAN SYSTEM OF GOVERNMENT....................... 1 50
TUCKERMAN'S AMERICA AND HER COMMENTATORS................ 2 50

POLITICAL ECONOMY.

BOWEN'S AMERICAN POLITICAL ECONOMY........................... 2 50
PERRY'S ELEMENTS OF POLITCIAL ECONOMY........................ 2 50
PERRY'S AN INTRODUCTION TO POLITICAL ECONOMY............. 1 50

RATIONALISM.

HURST'S HISTORY OF RATIONALISM................................... 3 50

RHETORIC AND ELOCUTION.

BAUTAIN'S ART OF EXTEMPORE SPEAKING............................ 1 50
DAY'S ART OF DISCOURSE... 1 50
McILVAINE'S ELOCUTION.. 1 75

SYNONYMS. (New Testament.)

TRENCH'S SYNONYMS OF THE NEW TESTAMENT, Part 1........ 1 25
TRENCH'S THE SAME. Part 2... 1 25

THEOLOGY.

GILLETT'S GOD IN HUMAN THOUGHT. 2 vols....................... 5 00
GILLETT'S MORAL SYSTEM.. 1 25
HODGE'S SYSTEMATIC THEOLOGY. 3 vols., with Index........... 12 00
PARKER'S PARACLETE... 2 00
VAN OOSTERZEE'S CHRISTIAN DOGMATICS, reduced to............. 5 00

The Speaker's Commentary on the Bible:

With an Explanatory and Critical Commentary, and a Revision of the Translation,

BY BISHOPS AND CLERGY OF THE ANGLICAN CHURCH.

EDITED BY

F. C. COOK, M. A., CANON OF EXETER.

Preacher at Lincoln's Inn, and Chaplain in Ordinary to the Queen.

THE OLD TESTAMENT.

Now complete, in Six Volumes, royal 8vo.

Half calf, $7.50; sheep, $6.50; cloth, $5.00 per volume.

Volume I.

GENESIS. Rt. Rev. E. H. BROWNE, Bishop of Ely, author of "Exposition of the XXXIX. Articles," etc.
EXODUS. Canon COOK and Rev. SAMUEL CLARK, author of "The Bible Atlas," etc.
LEVITICUS. Rev. SAMUEL CLARK.
NUMBERS. Canon ESPIN and Rev J. F. THRUPP.
DEUTERONOMY. Canon ESPIN, author of "Critical Essays."

Volumes II. and III.

JOSHUA. Canon ESPIN.
JUDGES, RUTH, SAMUEL. Rt. Rev. Lord ARTHUR HERVEY, Bishop of Bath and Wells, author of "Inspiration of the Holy Scriptures," etc.
KINGS, CHRONICLES, EZRA, NEHEMIAH, ESTHER. Canon RAWLINSON, author of "Five Great Monarchies of the Ancient East."

Volume IV.

JOB. Canon COOK.
PSALMS. Very Rev. G. H. JOHNSON, Dean of Wells, author of "Sermons preached in Wells Cathedral," and Rev. C. J. ELLIOTT.
PROVERBS. Rev. E. H. PLUMPTRE, author of "Christ and Christendom."
ECCLESIASTES. Rev. W. T. BULLOCK, Secretary to the S. P. G.
SONG OF SOLOMON Rev. T. KINGSBURY.

Volume V.

ISAIAH. Rev. Dr. W. KAY, author of "The Psalms translated from the Hebrew," etc.
JEREMIAH, LAMENTATIONS. R. PAYNE SMITH, D. D., Dean of Canterbury, author of "Bampton Lectures for 1869," etc.

Volume VI. *(Nearly ready.)*

EZEKIEL. Rev. Dr. G. CURREY, author of "Hulsean Lectures, 1851."
DANIEL. Archdeacon H. J. ROSE, author of "Sermons on the Duty of the Clergy," etc., and Rev. I. FULLER.
MINOR PROPHETS. Rev. E. HUXTABLE, Professor GANDELL, Rev. F. MEYRICK, Rev. S. CLARK, Rev. W. DRAKE.

*** The NEW TESTAMENT is in the Press.

Any or all of the volumes sent, post or express charges prepaid, on receipt of the price, by the publishers,

SCRIBNER, ARMSTRONG, AND COMPANY,

743 AND 745 BROADWAY, NEW YORK.

THREE IMPORTANT THEOLOGICAL WORKS.

THE PARACLETE

An Essay on the Personality and Ministry of the Holy Ghost, with some Reference to Current Discussions.

By JOSEPH PARKER, D.D., Author of "ECCE DEUS," etc. One vol., 12mo, cloth, ... $1.50

From the Church Journal.

"It is written in a warm, devout, earnest manner, with much power of reasoning and wealth of illustration, and very much suggestiveness, as though the author were rather burdened with the amount he had to say and used necessary repression. The introduction, and the essays reviewing Mr. Huxley, at the end, are perhaps the best parts of the book."

MODERN DOUBT AND CHRISTIAN BELIEF

A SERIES OF APOLOGETIC LECTURES ADDRESSED TO EARNEST SEEKERS AFTER TRUTH. By THEODORE CHRISTLIEB, University Preacher and Professor of Theology at Bonn. One vol., 8vo, cloth, ... $3.00

From the Presbyterian.

"One rises from the reading of this volume with mind and heart expanded and enriched, feeling that he has seen the gigantic and imposing structure of skepticism shattered and the solid rock of Divine truth disclosed. He knows not which to admire most — the author's wide and thorough research, the exhaustiveness of his discussion, his even-balanced and judicial impartiality, or his clear and finished style. Every minister and every lay student of theology needs the work, and no one who saw and heard its gifted author while in this country will need urging to procure it."

THE SUPERHUMAN ORIGIN OF THE BIBLE

INFERRED FROM ITSELF.

By HENRY ROGERS, Author of "THE ECLIPSE OF FAITH," etc. One vol. 12mo, cloth, ... $2.00

From the Congregationalist.

"Mr. ROGERS has constructed a volume which is to outlive all his other writings. It is an instructive, stimulating, well-compacted book. Most of the considerations which he has marshaled in proof of his thesis have been presented by others, some of them with greater fulness and equal brilliancy. He has brought together what has been scattered in many treatises. He has freshened familiar illustrations and welded into one many common proofs, so that they carry a new persuasiveness, and he has added not a few subtle and suggestive and most satisfactory illustrations of the wonderful nature of that Word which abideth."

The above books sent, postpaid, on receipt of the price, by the publishers,

SCRIBNER, ARMSTRONG & CO., NEW YORK.

THREE NEW VOLUMES
OF THE OLD TESTAMENT PORTION OF
Lange's Commentary.

I. SAMUEL, I. and II.
II. EZEKIEL and DANIEL.
III. CHRONICLES, EZRA, NEHEMIAH, and ESTHER.

There have been thus far issued of LANGE'S COMMENTARY, TWELVE VOLUMES on the Old Testament, and TEN on the New Testament, as follows:

OLD TESTAMENT VOLUMES.

I. GENESIS.
II. EXODUS and LEVITICUS.
III. JOSHUA, JUDGES, and RUTH.
IV. SAMUEL.
V. KINGS.
VI. CHRONICLES, EZRA, NEHEMIAH, and ESTHER.
VII. JOB.
VIII. PSALMS.
IX. PROVERBS, SONG OF SOLOMON, ECCLESIASTES.
X. EZEKIEL and DANIEL.
IX. JEREMIAH and LAMENTATIONS.
XII. THE MINOR PROPHETS.

In Preparation: — Numbers and Deuteronomy (1 vol.); Isaiah (1 vol.).

NEW TESTAMENT VOLUMES.

I. Matthew.
II. Mark and Luke.
III. John.
IV. Acts.
V. Romans.
VI. Corinthians.
VII. Galatians, Ephesians, Philippians, and Colossians.
VIII. Thessalonians, Timothy, Titus, Philemon, Hebrews.
IX. James, Peter, John, and Jude.
X. Revelation. With an Index to New Testament vols.

It will be observed that the New Testament portion is complete.

Each one vol. 8vo. Price per vol., in Cloth, $5.00; in Sheep, $6.50; in Half Calf, $7.50.

NAMES AND DENOMINATIONS OF CONTRIBUTORS.

W. G. T. SHEDD, D.D., Presbyterian.
E. A. WASHBURNE, D.D., Episcopal.
A. C. KENDRICK, D.D., Baptist.
W. H. GREEN, D.D., Presbyterian.
J. F. HURST, D.D., Methodist.
TAYLER LEWIS, LL.D., Dutch Refor'd.
REV. CH. F. SHAFFER, D.D., Lutheran.
R. D. HITCHCOCK, D.D., Presbyterian.
E. HARWOOD, D.D., Episcopal.
H. B. HACKETT, D.D., Baptist.
JOHN LILLIE, D.D., Presbyterian.
REV. W. G. SUMNER, Episcopal.
PROF. CHARLES ELLIOTT, Presbyt'n.
THOS. C. CONANT, D.D., Baptist.
E. D. YEOMANS, D.D., Presbyterian.
REV. C. C. STARBUCK, Congregational.
J. ISIDOR MOMBERT, D.D., Episcopal.
D. W. POOR, D.D., Presbyterian.
C. P. WING, D.D., Presbyterian.
GEORGE E. DAY, D.D., Congregational.
REV. P. H. STEENSTRA, Episcopal.
A. GOSMAN, D.D., Presbyterian.
PRES. CHAS. A. AIKEN, D.D., Presbyt'n.
M. B. RIDDLE, D.D., Dutch Reformed.
PROF. WM. WELLS, D.D., Methodist.
W. H. HORNBLOWER, D.D., Presbyt'n.
PROF. GEORGE BLISS, Baptist.
T. W. CHAMBERS, D.D., Reformed.

☞ Each volume of "LANGE'S COMMENTARY" is complete in itself, and can be purchased separately. Sent, post-paid, to any address upon receipt of the price ($5 per volume) by the publishers,

SCRIBNER, ARMSTRONG & CO., NEW YORK.

INVALUABLE TO THE STUDENT OF CHURCH HISTORY.

[A New Edition Reduced in Price.]

Dr. H. B. Smith's Chronological Tables

HISTORY OF THE CHURCH OF CHRIST, IN CHRONOLOGICAL TABLES:

A Synchronistic View of the Events, Characteristics, and Culture of each period, including the History of Polity, Worship, Literature, and Doctrines, together with two Supplementary Tables upon the Church in America; and an Appendix, containing the series of Councils, Popes, Patriarchs, and other Bishops, and a full Index.

BY THE LATE HENRY B. SMITH, D.D.,
Professor in the Union Theological Seminary of the City of New York.

REVISED EDITION.

One volume, folio cloth, *price reduced from $6.75 to $5.00.*

The title of this work, given above, will indicate its scope and purpose. It is a work that has cost its learned author an almost incredible amount of labor, and wonderfully does it facilitate the study of Church History. The plan of the work is unique and highly ingenious. The whole History of the Christian Church is divided into Ancient, Mediæval, and Modern; subdivided into six General Periods; and each Table has its limits defined by some signal event. The headings of each Table give, in a concise form, the main points that distinguish the Period and the Table. The first page in each Table contains three columns; the first column is a generalization of the events; the second contains as much of secular contemporaneous history as is necessary for the understanding of the history of the Church, and the third exhibits the state of literature, philosophy, and culture. The second page of each Table is devoted to the External history, the third and fourth to the Internal history of the Church. Ministers, students of theology, and all who desire a comprehensive knowledge of Church History will find this a highly valuable help.

Opinion of Rev. Dr. W. G T. SHEDD.

"*Prof. Smith's Historical Tables are the best that I know of in any language. . . In preparing such a work, with so much care and research, Prof. Smith has furnished to the student an apparatus that will be of lifelong service to him.*"

Opinion of Rev. Dr. WILLIAM ADAMS.

"*The labor expended upon such a work is immense, and its accuracy and completeness do honor to the research and scholarship of its author, and are an invaluable acquisition to our literature.*"

*** *The above work for sale by all Booksellers, or will be sent, express charges paid, on receipt of advertised price, by the Publishers,*

SCRIBNER, ARMSTRONG & CO.,
743 & 745 BROADWAY, NEW YORK.

[Authorized Edition printed from duplicate plates of the complete English Edition with all the illustrations.]

MEMOIR OF
NORMAN MACLEOD, D.D.,

Minister of Barony Parish, Glasgow; one of her Majesty's Chaplains, Dean of the Chapel Royal, etc.

BY HIS BROTHER, REV. DONALD MACLEOD, B.A.,
One of Her Majesty's Chaplains, Editor of
"Good Words," etc.

WITH STEEL PORTRAIT AND NUMEROUS ILLUSTRATIONS.

New and Cheaper Edition. Two volumes in one. Crown 8vo. Cloth, $2.50.

In less than a month after publication this Memoir reached a sale of SEVEN THOUSAND copies in Great Britain. It is one of the liveliest, most amusing, and at the same time most profitable of recent biographies.

The volume overflows with racy and characteristic Scotch anecdotes, while Dr. Macleod's irrepressible buoyancy of spirits sparkles on every page and now and then breaks out in pen and ink caricatures, suggestive of THACKERAY in his best vein.

CRITICAL NOTICES.

From the Atlantic Monthly.

"The life of Dr. Macleod is one of the most interesting and affecting biographies of a year singularly prolific in important memoirs. It is written by his brother, the Rev. Donald Macleod, and is beautifully written, with great tenderness, and at the same time a most dignified restraint of eulogy."

From the New York Observer.

"To a remarkable list of interesting memoirs of prominent men that have appeared within the last twelve months is now added the one of which the title is given above. The relations of Dr. Macleod, not only to the religious and literary public, but to the royal household, his prominence as a man of talent and influence, and his genial character, have awakened expectations in regard to his biography that will not be disappointed."

From the Advance.

"A very enjoyable and instructive book we have found it to be, in the variety of its contents, and in the insight which it has given us unto the heart of a very noble Christian."

From the Christian Union.

"We would commend the book as one in which no person whose heart is in the right place can fail to be greatly interested."

From the Christian Intelligencer.

"There is something very refreshing and invigorating in the memoirs of such a man as Dr. Macleod."

From the New York "Evening Post."

"The work is one of uncommon interest."

Sent post paid on receipt of price by the publishers,

SCRIBNER, ARMSTRONG & CO.,
743 & 745 BROADWAY, NEW YORK.

[A companion volume to Conybeare and Howson's St. Paul.]

The Life and Writings of Saint John.

BY THE

Rev. JAMES M. MACDONALD, D.D.,

PRINCETON, NEW JERSEY.

Edited, with an INTRODUCTION, *by the*

Very Rev. J. S. HOWSON, D.D., Dean of Chester,

Joint Author of CONYBEARE AND HOWSON'S ST. PAUL.

In one large handsome volume 8vo. Cloth. Price, $5.00.

LIST OF FULL-PAGE ILLUSTRATIONS AND MAPS, ENGRAVED EXPRESSLY FOR THIS WORK.

Bust of Augustus.	Shechem.	Bust of Nero.	Sardis.
Bust of Tiberius Cæsar.	Cæsarea Philippi.	Thyatira.	Site of Capernaum.
Bethsaida, Site of.	Garden of Gethsemane.	Philadelphia.	Jacob's Well.
Jerusalem.	Bethany.	Laodicea,	Tiberias.
Cana of Galilee.	Samaria.	Bust of Julius Cæsar.	Pool of Siloam.
Road from Jerusalem to Jericho.	Bust of Caligula.	Old Tyre,	Bust of Vespasian.
Jerusalem, Walls of	Ephesus.	Bust of Titus.	Smyrna.
	St. John.	Pergamos.	
Imperium Romanorum Latissime Patens.		Palestine in Time of Christ. Asia Minor, showing the Seven Churches	Patmos. St. John's Travels.

TABLE OF CONTENTS.

I. The Place in History, and character of the period in which the Apostle John appeared.
II. Parentage, early life, and natural traits of the Apostle.
III. St. John in his early stage of preparation for the Apostleship as a disciple of John the Baptist.
IV. St. John under the training of the Great Master Himself from the beginning of His public ministry.
V. Preparation for his work from intercourse and instruction in private; especially from the great sacrifice offered by Jesus, as witnessed by the Apostle himself.
VI. Crowning proof of the Messiahship of Jesus, as witnessed by St. John.
VII. History of St. John in the Acts of the Apostles.
VIII. Later History from traditionary sources, till his arrival at Ephesus, and banishment to Patmos.
IX. St. John writes the Apocalypse. Its Date and Design.
X. Analysis of the Apocalypse, with brief explanatory Notes.
XI. Traditionary History of the Apostle continued.
XII. St. John writes the Fourth Gospel. Date, Design, and Contents.
XIII. Analysis of the Gospel, with brief explanatory Notes.
XIV. Last days and concluding Writings of the Apostle.
XV. Analysis of the Epistles, with brief explanatory Notes.

*** *The above work for sale by all booksellers, or will be sent, post or express charges paid, upon receipt of advertised price by the publishers,*

SCRIBNER, ARMSTRONG & CO.,

743 & 745 BROADWAY, NEW YORK.

The Great Theological Work of the Age.

DR. HODGE'S THEOLOGY.

Systematic Theology.

By CHARLES HODGE, D.D., LL.D.,
of Princeton Theological Seminary.

Three volumes 8vo., including Index, ... $12.00.

In these volumes are comprised the results of the life-long labors and investigations of one of the most eminent theologians of the age. The work covers the ground usually occupied by treatises on Systematic Theology, and adopts the commonly received divisions of the subject,—THEOLOGY, Vol. I.; ANTHROPOLOGY, Vol. II.; SOTERIOLOGY AND ESCHATOLOGY, Vol. III.

The INTRODUCTION is devoted to the consideration of preliminary matters, such as Method, or the principles which should guide the student of Theology, and the different theories as to the source and standard of our knowledge of divine things, Rationalism, Mysticism, the Roman Catholic doctrine of the Rule of Faith, and the Protestant doctrine on that subject.

The department of THEOLOGY proper includes the origin of the Idea of God, the Being of God, the Anti-Theistic systems of Atheism, Polytheism, Materialism, and Pantheism; the Nature of God, the Divine Attributes, the Doctrines of the Trinity, the Divinity of Christ, and of the Holy Spirit; the Decrees of God, Creation, Providence, and Miracles.

The department of ANTHROPOLOGY includes the Nature, Origin, and Antiquity of Man, his Primitive State and Probation; the Fall; the Effect of Adam's Sin upon himself and upon his Posterity; the Nature of Sin; the Different Philosophical and Theological Theories on that subject.

SOTERIOLOGY includes the Plan or Purpose of God in reference to the Salvation of Men; the Person and Work of the Redeemer; his Offices as Prophet, Priest, and King; the Work of the Holy Spirit in applying the redemption purchased by Christ; Common and Efficacious Grace, Regeneration, Faith, Justification, Sanctification, the Law or Rule of Life, and the means of Grace.

ESCHATOLOGY includes the State of the Soul after Death; the Second Coming of Christ; the Resurrection of the Body; the General Judgment and End of the World, and the Doctrines concerning Heaven and Hell.

The plan of the author is to state and vindicate the teachings of the Bible on these various subjects, and to examine the antagonistic doctrines of different classes of Theologians. His book, therefore, is intended to be both didactic and elenchtic.

The various topics are discussed with that close and keen analytical and logical power, combined with that simplicity, lucidity, and strength of style which have already given Dr. HODGE a world-wide reputation as a controversialist and writer, and as an investigator of the great theological problems of the day.

Single copies sent post-paid on receipt of the price.

SCRIBNER, ARMSTRONG & CO.,

New York.

Popular and Standard Books

PUBLISHED BY
SCRIBNER, ARMSTRONG & CO.,
743 and 745 Broadway, New York,
In 1876.

BRYANT and GAY'S Popular History of the United States. VOLUME I. PROFUSELY ILLUSTRATED. (Sold only by subscription). 8vo, extra cloth.................... $5 00
Blackie's (Prof. John Stuart) Songs of Religion and Life. Sq. 12mo............... 1 50
Bible Commentary. Vol. VI. Ezekiel, Daniel and the Minor Prophets. 8vo...... 5 00
Brooks' (Noah) The Boy Emigrants. *Illustrated*, 12mo 1 50
Bushnell. (*Uniform edition of the select works of Horace Bushnell, D.D.*) Christian Nurture. 12mo. Sermons for the New Life. 12mo. Christ and His Salvation, 12mo. Each... 1 50
Cahun's (Leon) Adventures of Captain Mago. PROFUSELY ILLUSTRATED. Cr. 8vo.... 2 50
Dodge's (Mrs. M. M.) Theophilus and Others, 12mo............................... 1 50
Dwight's (Dr. B. W.) Modern Philology. *Cheap Edition*. 2 vols. cr. 8vo....... 4 00
EPOCHS OF MODERN HISTORY. Edited by E. E. MORRIS, M.A., and others. Creighton's Age of Elizabeth. *With five maps*. Hale's Fall of the Stuarts, *With two maps*. Gardiner's Puritan Revolution. *With four maps*. Stubb's Early Plantagenets. *With two maps*. Each 1 vol. sq. 12mo, cloth................ 1 00
EPOCHS OF ANCIENT HISTORY. Edited by G. W. Cox, M.A., and others. Cox's Greeks and Persians. *With four maps*. Capes' Early Roman Empire. *With two maps*. Cox's Athenian Empire from the Flight of Xerxes to the Fall of Athens. *With five maps*. Each 1 vol. sq. 12mo, cloth................. 1.00
Field's (Dr. Henry M.) From the Lakes of Killarney to the Golden Horn. 12mo..... 2 00
Gilbert's (W. S.) Original Plays. 12mo.. 1 75
Holland's (Dr. J. G.) Every Day Topics: A Book of Briefs. 12mo................ 1 75
—— The Mistress of the Manse. *Illustrated edition*. Small 4to............... 5 00
Hale's (Rev. Edward Everett) Philip Nolan's Friends. *Illustrated*. 12mo..... 1 75
Jernigham Journals (The). *Two vols. in one*. 12mo............................ 1 25
—— (Author of) Miss Hitchcock's Wedding Dress. 12mo......................... 1 25
LANGE'S COMMENTARY. Dr. PHILIP SCHAFF, General Editor. Exodus and Leviticus. Ezekiel and Daniel. Chronicles, Ezra, Nehemiah and Esther. Each one vol. 8vo... 5 00
Memoir of Norman Macleod, D.D., by his brother, Rev. DONALD MACLEOD, M.A. *Illustrated*. 2 vols. 8vo.. 4 50
Plato's Best Thoughts, as compiled from Prof. JOWETT'S Translation. 8vo....... 2 50
Parker's (Dr. Joseph). The Paraclete. *New and cheaper edition*. 12mo........ 1 50
SANS-SOUCI SERIES (THE). Edited by RICHARD HENRY STODDARD. Haydon's (B. R.) Life, Letters and Table Talk. *Illustrated* Men and Manners in America One Hundred Years Ago. *Illustrated*. An Anecdote Biography of Percy B. Shelley. *Illustrated*. Each 1 vol. sq. 12mo................................... 1 50
Schuyler's (Eugene) Turkistan. *With three maps and numerous illustrations*, 2 vols 8vo.. 5 00
Stanley's (Dean) Lectures on the History of the Jewish Church. *Third Series*. 8vo. 4 00
Ueberweg's History of Philosophy. *New and cheaper edition*. 2 vols. 8vo...... 5 00
Van Oosterzee's Christian Dogmatics. *New and cheaper edition*. 2 vols. 8vo.... 5 00
Verne's (Jules) Mysterious Island. Three vols. in one. *Illustrated*........... 3 00
—— Michael Strogoff. *Illustrated*. Cr. 8vo.................................. 3 00

Any or all of the above sent, post or express charges paid, on receipt of the price by the publishers.